# PELLETIER CHRONICLES

## - 500 YEARS

*By Lonnie Pelletier*

Cover design by Lonnie Pelletier
Editing by Martha Todd
Instar Publishing Inc.

Author:      Pelletier, Lonnie, 1943
Title:       Pelletier Chronicles - 500 Years
ISBN:        978-1-928151-13-5
Subjects:

             1. Pelletier family.
             2. Canada - - Genealogy
             3. France - - Genealogy

# PELLETIER CHRONICLES - 500 YEARS

## PART I - Their history

## PART II - My personal involvement

*It is with great pride in family that I dedicate this book to Pelletiers throughout the world. As a child I did not know the Pelletiers; and may this book provide insight such that others need not be as unaware.*

# PELLETIER CHRONICLES - 500 YEARS

## PART I - Their History

# PART I - Their History

## Chapter 1 - Historic Beginnings

"I know exactly how I got into this vegetable bin. Actually, I know more than just the way I crawled in. My mother told me that we always looked our worst when we were slithering into hiding, like a snake seeing something moving that could do it harm.

We women always had a place to hide. It was that, or being mounted by the lord of the manor - -or one of his uppity ne'er-do-wells. They were rough when they rode you. A good woman could always count on a slap or two on the face, whether she liked it or not – even after delivering the goods.

What I hated most was when they took your sex in front of your family. I hated that. But then, that is life – and in life there are those above you and well, sometimes there are those below you. It is a curse to be a bit of a beautiful woman, even an older one like me. It's a fact of life that those above you also want to be in you. That's my experience, and that's why I'm hiding in this bin.

There is a war outside and it doesn't seem to matter which side those fighting knights are on. When they see those of us lower than themselves, they take. That's why we women always had to have a place to hide.

I told my grandson René to get out of here. Chartres is no place for a lad like him. He works hard, but he prefers to stare out at the trees and ponds. He is not a very good servant of the church, or of God or of our country. He likes to think too much. When the fighting stops, maybe I'll talk to him again. I'm the oldest in the Pelletier family now. The rest, well, they're all dead from work. They should all leave now. I've heard that there are better places – and cleaner places. Where people are not animals. I've heard that people can grow all that they want up in the hills. Nobody is raped and nobody is beaten. My family should all leave.

If the Huguenot army wins this battle, I'll be okay, I guess. I'm an old lady and they won't bother me anymore. If the Huguenots get beaten back, I'll still survive. I sold all of my carrots last week. I can be eating all winter, at least this time. Anyway it unfolds its okay. I've got vegetables to eat here. It's dark in here, but I've got vegetables. I'll just wait until I don't hear anymore horses and cannon.

I have to stay here in Chartres. I'm too old to make a new home somewhere else - but my kin should all leave. I guess I was born in a year before one thousand and five hundred. The priest told me that was important. Either way I'm just feeling old. My body gets stiff and sore when I'm scrunched up like this.

I once hid away from the lord of the manor's son for three days. I hid on top of a haystack. He had seen me at the marketplace. My good husband could have fought him, but he would have been killed – or worse yet, we would have lost our right to toil on the land we had been allowed on. All of us should just leave. I'll be talking to my grandson, René."

\* \* \*

René Pelletier was about to achieve his goal for the day. Three more kilometres and he would be within a half-day's walk of Bresolettes. He had left Chartres just over one week before. In retrospect he thought that the journey hadn't been too bad. Once he'd started away from the valley he had felt much safer. In the final outcome, the Huguenots had been well defeated even after they were inside the walls of Chartres, but it wasn't them he was worried about. It was the reality of life – most often those with horses and armour took from those on foot. He walked along his planned route knowing that there were no bandits on this trail - just hardworking people like himself.

Leaving Chartres had been difficult for this soft spoken young man. He hadn't planned on the tears from his family. But he might have expected it, as the Pelletier family had always shown their love for each other, no matter what. The village of

Chartres itself wasn't difficult to leave. René hadn't given it too much thought, but he knew that a number of issues relative to the 1500s and earlier were dominant.

The major impetus was the School of Chartres. By its very existence, the Chartres Notre-Dame Cathedral had created a hierarchy or class system that dominated the town. Firstly it had been built to be the "greatest" cathedral in France. As a patron of the most sublime of twelfth and thirteenth-century art, it was to symbolize the incredible power of the bishops of Chartres between 1134 and 1260 - when it had been rebuilt. Fires had devastated it; as it had proved itself vulnerable like everything else. Three hundred local workmen rebuilt it in record time, with the hardships and ramifications of life and death being sporadically recorded through the process.

The 172 stained glass windows were dynamic enough to be considered among the finest in Europe. Within their design, the caste system of the town was again reinforced to all of its citizens. The heraldic arms of "great" families, along with the specific work-guilds, were shown in detail.

The townspeople of Chartres all held the same rigidity of thought. The better homes were near the top plateau along with the church. Below were ramps and staircases down to each of the plateaus of the medieval trades-people. Whether it was the plateaus for the water carriers, or that of the carpenters, their level was dependent on the whims of the church hierarchy.

This was all in proportion to the necessity of the trade, as it was related in importance to the church- building process. The Eure River wound very casually through the town; however it was the walls built near the river that were more of a dividing line and a sought-after area for housing. To be housed on the upper area meant protection from raids of warriors. To be on the outside meant total vulnerability. Each geographical level of height of their homes meant a defined change in both status and safety for every inhabitant.

René's Pelletier family were not a part of the worshiping process that existed at the main cathedral. Five other churches were provided for their "lesser type", each with its own class designation. This again meant a stratified community for even the balance of these worshipers. Also known to all was the undisputed "Christian Doctrine of the Chartres Schools". This gave the bishops a complete mandate even over those chosen by the king to be lords or counts.

René could not have foreseen that the church would control here with adamant rule up until the French Revolution that would follow in the future. Until then, only the family of the Count of Chartres would be allowed to worship at the ancient Saint Aignan parish. Two hundred and fifty years later, after its erection in 1541, the Revolutionaries would use churches such as this almost symbolically. The village of Chartres stood for all that they wanted to eliminate – relative to individual freedom. The Saint Aignan church would ironically become a prison and then an animal fodder shop. It was in this stratified environment of sixteenth-century Chartres that René had grown to be a young man and he would have loved to know, of this use of democracy that would not transpire for more than two hundred years. As he journeyed on, what René did know was that he would enjoy the solitude of life in Bresolettes and its forests, away from the chaos, the local class system and the wars.

The Huguenots had attacked in 1568, and twenty years later there had been a major revolution in Paris. High property taxes here had fostered the creation of the cantilevered second-floor home over the walkways, as these taxes were in ratio to the measured amount of only the ground level living.

The river had overflowed its banks, which caused strife for the workmen living near it. The largest bridge was on Rue de Bourgand and it was in desperate need of repair. The backs of the workmen would again be used. Had René stayed he would have been one of those workers. He would have been paid in bread, not tradable commodities.

René had said his goodbyes in Chartres and left. It was still the century of opportunity with what was considered to be new and exciting knowledge. However, René could not write, and he could only read a little. "He would make sure that he would have a son. That son would be able to read – and that son would be able to write." He promised himself that, almost thinking aloud, as he prepared a mattress of leaves over the ground from which he had cleared branches away. One more night sleeping under the trees and he would be at his goal and destination.

He had chosen Bresolettes for only one reason. He had seen a map that had been sketched of the Perche forest. Bresolettes was depicted as being on a hill beside a lake, and it was the highest village around. René knew that his decision wasn't entirely logical, but he reasoned that in Chartres he had lived on the lowest point of land; and in Bresolettes he might be on the highest. The village itself was even on the highest ground above the small lake – and to René, that was a desirable and achievable choice. Goals however were not really a part of his thought pattern, but survival in these times meant that choices often dictated life or death. As he let sleep take over his thoughts, he again made a vow. *Somehow his family would have choices in the future.* In Chartres there had been none.

It was interesting then to note that as life later evolved for René, he married and had a son, and it was his grandson who had made major choices. In René's time though, it followed that no church in the world could have been designed more differently from the cathedral of Our Lady of Chartres - than the church that these villagers of Bresolettes had built for themselves. In that, their choice in local church design would survive for many centuries.

As a boy, René had watched the chanting pilgrims carrying their gifts as they climbed the winding streets to pay homage to the Queen of Heaven in her terrestrial palace. Henry IV had come here to be crowned. At that time it had had been widely acknowledged as a city of contemporary learning. But to René it was a city of long days of hard work and enslavement, with a required dedication serving the religious order of the masters over him.

It was largely because of the Hundred Year's War that the city walls of Chartres had to be strengthened, and in 1356 a moat had been dug out as an extra defence. Nine gates then existed. The wars had been as consistent as the labour.

René was still remembering the reason his grandmother had often hidden in the stone and mud vegetable storage bin. She was now in her seventies and was a small, frail, but very willowy elderly lady. Her explanation for staying on, amid the turmoil, was that it was still her home, and that when she was to die she would die in it. No one would ever question this lady, set in her ways and proud of who she was to her last days. She had survived the siege by eating some of the vegetables that she had been lying on, while ignoring normal bodily processes.

Solid rock walls had been built around the inner world and hierarchy of the cathedral. Being a widow; her meagre home was not protected by these walls. The walls were on the hill, far above her physically, and high above her social status mentally. The Vikings had attacked over the centuries and the stories of their onslaught, handed down to her through a few generations, were not stories to be relished. As the elderly woman hid, the Huguenot army was driven out of the walled city of Chartres in their final moments of the war. This story of her survival would become the one that she would enjoy telling most.

There had been nothing grand or ceremonial about that which later was to be referred to by many naïve writers as the grandeur of the Chartre's epoch. Having been born just before the turn of the 1500's though, and coupled with that great pride that never seemed to be stolen from her, she knew that her grandson would go onto a better life. This, then, was the chronicle that was to begin a story of a family. Perhaps it could be said that the family chronicle began in a stone and mud vegetable storage bin. There is no glamour in that, but here is a quiet pride in survival that lives on with the passage of centuries.

She had told René the stories of men with coins from the *Exchange Road* in Chartres, who until 1464 had stood at their benches. The French word for benches is *banc* and it is the origin of the word "bank". She had taught him how, when they were referred to as *banquiers* (bench-men), they would exchange locally minted coinage of the Count of Chartres, for the commodities from farm lands. In describing the more secluded lives she knew she was creating an image for him - a dream of a more rural and peaceful region, where he could be involved in those farmlands.

As the feudal system had declined, there had been a drifting away from the rural land toward the developing towns, some of which were becoming increasingly important as trading centres. That had brought the Pelletier family into Chartres in a prior time. There, awestruck, they had found the main cathedral with its complete collection of medieval stained glass. It formed an incomparable record of life and faith in the Middle Ages. Set like enormous transparent illuminated manuscripts in walls of limestone, the panels depicted kings and princes and great ladies of the court, in fine silks and ermine and cloth of spungold. There they gazed upon knights in coats of mail and priests shown in richly embroidered vestments of ruby, saffron, azure and emerald.

But this was not reality. They also saw images of hooded peasants in smocks of coarse cloth, or stripped to the waist and standing as proud men ready for harder toil. Artisans were shown with their tools in hand as they sculpted, wove or carved. Just as unreal were the fishmongers beneath beautiful and coloured umbrellas. Still others are shown proudly displaying their earthly wares for sale.

To believe this display was typical of life during the Middle Ages would be more than a little disrespectful of those who survived to live a full life. This masquerade of colour was not a part of their existence. It was for this reason that the villagers did not care about their social exclusion, for it was not an exclusion of a tangible life. In later years, those same windows could be said to be propaganda material, an illusion of *smoke and mirrors*. Much of this would explain why, during French Revolution, there was much degrading of this type of structure. The history and destiny of Chartres, was always a dual separated track. Its people, separate from its cathedral, were never and will never be, interwoven, in any positive sense.

The names of the streets in Chartres indicated the trades that took place on their cobbled stones. These were the French language equivalents of streets of: the money changers, the herbs sellers, the shoemakers, the fishmongers and the coopers. Throughout this period, artists were allowed (by the church), to have a very slow evolution of freedom, to create paintings that were not entirely focused on superficial church life and specific saintly lives.

In 1588, it became "the turn" of King Henry III of France to hide in Chartres. He had fled Paris after what has become known as the *Day of the Barricades*. Unfortunately (or fortunately) he had other digs far removed from the vegetable bin. As the king did not arrive quietly, by most reasoning in the village, they would be attacked. It was now a logical time for the departure of René and his friends to a more peaceful rural region of France.

René may have lived in one of the washer houses, or even at the back of a wool or leather mill. As a single labourer his needs were not many. Packing was easy. Transportation was by foot. One shirt could be wrapped around all his other clothing, and this could be tied on a strap over his back. With a walking stick, all that was important could be carried without impeding his pace of a slow walk. A wide-brimmed hat, an off-white shirt, his leather hide jacket and warm wool trousers made up his wardrobe. As a robust young man he wore no sweater and his shirt was opened wide, as if to demonstrate his invulnerability.

The Pelletier family had turned up in history throughout the west and southwest of Paris. In 1294, Jeanle Pelletier had been given the vague currency amount of a *Round Stamp of 38,000*, along with a parcel of land, by the king. This was a form of royal promise done by investiture, which in feudal law is the delivery of possession of land, in the presence of witnesses. The land was near Rouen, near the abbey of Jumièges – within the interior of an arch in the Seine River, near the river bend that forms six star shapes.

In 1504, at Loudin, Francois le Pelletier had taken an investigation, also called a toll, on behalf of the king. It was from there that René's grandmother's family had moved north to Chartres. None of the moves were of any great distance; and they were solely about survival.

Like that of many workmen the world over, René's arrival in the community of Bresolettes was without fanfare. He arrived and settled-in unnoticed even by his wife-to-be. René was not able to obtain the use of a farm; that privilege was to be to his son, Eloi's. Eloi did learn to read and write and it was the home of Eloi that would survive some four hundred years into the future. It was through the seigneurial system, in these peaceful hills, that life had been improved within three generations.

There were fourteen seigneuries under the king's rule bestowed upon the Pelletier family - over a period of two centuries. However neither Eloi, nor his father René nor his son Guillaume, had been a recipient. Such things were at the whim of the court and the reigning king's fancy.

The fourteen seigneuries granted, were:
1. Le Pelletier de Glatigny,
2. Le Pelletier de Glatigny Voir,
3. Le Pelletier de La Houssaye,
4. Le Pelletier de Liancourt,
5. Le Pelletier de Martainville,
6. Le Pelletier de Morfontaine,
7. Le Pelletier de Rosanbo Voir,
8. Le Pelletier de St Fargeau,
9. Le Pelletier de Woillemont,
10. Le Pelletier de Des Forts,
11. Le Pelletier des Tourelles,
12. Le Pelletier du Clary,
13. Le Pelletier de Beuze,
14. Le Pelletier du St. Remy (on *the island* of Martinique),

Can one ascertain that one's own family is not of Le Pelletier origin? The answer is that they cannot be certain. One can only hope to be of the family that, in effect, began in a vegetable bin. In that, it seems much more wholesome - and verification is easily valid, as any dispute from anyone else is very unlikely.

As posterity would have it, none of these seigneurial families would have been allowed to hold land in France, after the French Revolution. Also, none of this line remained farmers in France. There is therefore reason to conclude that the Canadian family branch, with hard labour as a way of life, had logically initiated the beginning of their Canadian odyssey.

For this particular Pelletier family, the elderly grandmother's birth, at the close of the fifteenth century, marked the beginning of their Renaissance. The Dark Ages were long behind them. By 1600, the population of France was over sixteen million people, but this was also the time of the rise of French Absolutism, with the impoverished peasantry paying most of the taxes. Wars and mobs were harsh and consistent in the town centres. The atmosphere of the rural area of the ancient province of Perche gave René and his new family the best life possible.

Emile was born January 28, 1899 at St. John, New Brunswick. On January 29, he was baptized Paul-Emile Pelletier, in St. Francois de Madawaska.

Emile Zola was one of the most famous writers in the French language, and as a tough- minded critic of French society, he had often immersed himself into both the political and humanistic issues of the day. To be named Emile in 1899, even when living in a provincial country outside of France, was to be a subject of great expectations.

*Naturalism* in literature was a term used by Emile Zola to describe heredity and environmental influence on human motivation and behavior. Within this format, if a writer wishes to depict life as it really is or was, both the character's thoughts and actions must be shown. Unlike *Realism* as a literary style, which also seeks to represent human life as it is actually lived, *Naturalism* connects itself to the philosophical doctrine of biological and social determinism, according to which human beings are devoid of free will. This concept of the absence of individual free will is what characterizes the lives of both Emile Pelletier and his distant forebear Guillaume.

In 1901 Emile Pelletier and his family moved to the Coleman, Alberta area, where one of his brothers and one of his sisters was born. In 1904 his father Stanley took Emile and his siblings to New Brunswick, where they were enrolled at the Convent in St. Basil. Somehow Emile felt Western Canadian, however, it was in a real sense that after twelve years of schooling in St. Basil he could not help but become imbued with Eastern Canadian sensibilities. As an individual, he would never quite establish his personal identity one way or the other.

Private Emile Pelletier had a nickname, as did many of these young soldiers in World War I. He was simply called *Kid Pelletier.* His older brother had called him *Kid* and it carried on. A nickname was many things. For one, it was a sign of masculine kinship. As soon as he had finished what was then the equivalent of high school, Emile had joined his father in the west. After a short visit he could now join the army. Education was important to his father, and as a longtime single parent, he was expecting that his son would adhere to wishes of schooling first.

His twelve years at the convent had produced in Emile a high degree of fluency in both French and English. This would prove later to be a great asset during his World War I travels. He had been as anxious and naïve as many others in his willingness to go to war. Emile's brother Art had also joined the army in Calgary, Alberta, where he initially worked at the administration offices, before finally being shipped out to the front lines of the Eastern front in Russia. Art had also become excited at the prospect of fighting for the city to be later called Leningrad. The inevitable burning and the partial destruction of that city along with the battle that he experienced were under its former, and ever changing, city name of Petrograd.

Emile had volunteered, serving in the 31$^{st}$ battalion out of Calgary. They would later become known as *Bell's Bulldogs,* at least as stated in their association directory. Many members despised the cliché for being unrealistic and sardonic relative to the theatre of war, but they were young men doing what they were expected to do. These expectations, however, were in stark contrast with the little information that they actually had been given. The excerpts from Emile's diary reveal lightheartedness, with denial of the brutal daily facts of both life and death.

He began by stating, *"Pte. E. P. Pelletier, No. 3207008,"* and he then told of his whereabouts.

*"I enlisted in Edmonton, Alberta, the 21$^{st}$ of March and reached Calgary the 23$^{rd}$. Left Calgary for England the 2$^{nd}$ of May. Reached Halifax the 8$^{th}$ and left there on the 10$^{th}$. Reached England the 23$^{rd}$ and landed in London the 24$^{th}$ of May. Was quarantined in a Segregation Camp at Frensham Pond until the 19$^{th}$ of July when I entered Bramshot Camp with the 21$^{st}$ Reserve Battalion.*

*Left Bramshott Camp after being fully trained for France on the 3$^{rd}$ of August. Reached Dover the 4$^{th}$ and on the 5$^{th}$ embarked.*

*"On the 5$^{th}$ we landed at Boulonge. After two days we took the train to Etaples. Two days later left on another train for Agnes les Duisans. Left it after a week on a march to join the 31$^{st}$ Battalion through Arras, Wancourt, then Marquion, and Haynecourt where we joined them. From there we went to Wasnes au bac in close supports for two days. Then we went to Monchecourt, for three weeks after which we left for the lines at Denain, and Valenciennes."*

Such was the terse, sketchy summary of a bloody hell at Wasnes Aubac, Denain, and Valenciennes, France, yet the diaries made it sound like a stroll through the countryside. Perhaps this was merely a survival mechanism. Through all of this, Private Emile Pelletier did what his comrades in arms did to relieve their own sanity. He copied both the letters from home and the letters sent home into a small book the same size as his diary. Little did he know that generations to follow would read these copies of the letters with awe. Emile's correspondence from his brother Art was regular and personal, and Emile did not often return the favour. His correspondence book goes on:

*"From Art, June 24, 1918. Received your letter kid, most welcome and am very glad to hear from you so often (you know what I mean, the opposite). Well kid since you went away everything is about the same with me, except that we moved to Sarcee Army Camp, just outside of Calgary, a couple of days after you left, and then we moved back downtown again a month later. Now we are still downtown but in a second house. No use giving you the address, I might have moved from here when you come back.*

*"Well I'm glad you made the trip O.K. and that you transferred into something else. Did they all have to transfer into something else or just those that wanted to? I have not*

been to Coleman yet, since February. I see somebody from the house once in awhile. About half the town of Coleman is moved up here. Gee there's a bunch of them around. There's 1500 Dough Boys gone last week, the first to go since you went. Yesterday 1200 USA. soldiers went through here on their way to England. They stopped in town for about six hours. They played a game of baseball against Calgary. The score was three each - it was a pretty good game.

"Papa is going to Pouce Coupe in a couple of days. He is passing through here Wednesday. That means that I'll have to get up about 6 o'clock to meet him at the station.

"Well kid, how is things in England? Tell me just what you think of it – if it's nicer than Canada or not and how are the fellows over there. I remembered you to McGregor and he wants to be remembered back to you, and he also wants to know what you think of the English girls. Don't forget to write often. I will do my best to write about every week and wish you would do the same. I heard Papa received your letter and I guess he'll tell you about the folks at home. Gooda bye. Art.

"From Art, July 12, 1918. Received three letters from you altogether and this is my second one to you although it is not very long since I wrote the last one first before (whatever that means).

"Well kid, glad to hear from you so often, and hope you keep it up. I haven't had a letter from the sisters since I put on the uniform. I just wrote to little sister Yvonne and gave her hell because she writes so often. I told her it was wasting stamps too much for her age, and in the same letter I gave her a hint to write to you pretty often. Whether she will is a different thing altogether. I haven't been to Coleman yet, but am expecting to get about two weeks off next month, but then again expecting and going is different, however all I can do is to wait and see what will happen. Uncle George was in town again last week for two or three days, and so was Annie Pisony – but Annie is like nothing to me now, she is still in town and I was supposed to go with her tonight, but I found an excuse saying I had to go back to work, and it worked alright, instead of being out at work I am drawing these few words to your ladyship (not even knowing what kind of ship that is) but it means you.

"McGregor is just the same as usual. I told him he had your permission to write to you and he said he was going to think it over. John Brennan was in town for the 1st of July with a bunch of other Scotchmen from Coleman. I saw Agnes Pelletier.

"Well kid hope you are getting letters once in awhile. I know if I was in your place I'd like to receive letters. Write as often as you like – you don't have to pay for stamps anyway.

"From Art, August 19, 1918. Received a letter from you a couple of days ago and am always glad to hear from you. Well kid since writing to you last, I have been visiting the old burg Coleman, for about twelve days. I stayed that long, not because I liked the place very, or the girls either, they are a hell of a looking bunch around that part of the earth aren't they, but you see I'm not very much struck on work so I thought I might as well have a few days more if I could, and I did. I was in Pincher Creek for one whole afternoon, everybody were asking how you was and also (I might just as well put it down while I think about it). Miss Vanlarkin told me to tell thee that she sends her BEST love. Say kid you should have seen the tears of joy spring to her face when I was telling her you were well and still thinking of her. But changement de propos, everybody is fine at the house.

"Levite wishes to be remembered to you. Gee I think the kid's voice has changed a lot since the last time I saw the little shrimp. He's got a regular man's voice now... Eva is just the same as before and so is grandma and Uncle Fred.... I suppose you know that daddy bought a team and lots of other kinds of Machinery, and I think he's getting some stock. I wish the hell I could help the old man. I can't save a darn cent to send to him, and I know you can't either unless you assign $15.00 of your pay. I think I'm getting a raise of 75 cents per day, and then I'll be able to send Daddy some. Gee if I went back to work at my old job in Coleman I could get over $4.00 a day. I was working there two days while I was on my holidays and they gave me $8.00. I don't know whether I earned them or not, anyway I got them and it sure came in handy... Well kid by your letters I see you did not get very much of our mail but I think you'll start getting some, one of these days alright. Auntie Edith writes to you about every other week and I almost do that too. In Pincher, Agnes was telling me she received a letter from your majesty, she was tickled about it too.

"Well I don't remember ever writing such a long letter in my life before, but I don't know, I kind of felt like it tonight. Keep up the writing old kid, even if it isn't a long letter you write, send something anyway. Art

"From Art, September 1, 1918. Just a few lines this time to tell you almost the same thing as before. Did not receive a letter from you which I suppose you didn't send, for about a month now, but am hoping that I'll get one soon. I'm always the same, Jake, and doing the same kind of work. All the rest of the family are fine too, as far as I know. I have not heard from Dad for quite a little while, but I presume he's well too.

"Gee I laughed a couple of days ago. I got a letter from our sisters and they want me to send some cash, they heard that I had so much money that I didn't know what to do with it, and seeing that I wasn't married, although it was about time I was, they said I ought to send them some of my dough. Now what do you think about that? I wonder who reported such good news to them. I don't believe the army is much of a place for a person to get floating in money par dessus la tîle eh?

"What do you think, I saw your friend Annie Vanlarkin again a couple of days ago. She asked me to remind you of her. I'm afraid this is a sad case between you two. However she might get over it. If you ever feel like writing to the kid make the address to Mount Royal College. I am enclosing herewith a snap, which I didn't know what to do with, that we had taken when I was at Coleman. Well kid write often, for people often inquire from me, how you is. Art

*"From Art, September 25, 1918. Received your letter a few days ago in which you mention having received two of mine. You know which one I mean, don't you? Well kid I'm always Jake, and as far as I know so is the rest of the family... I'm still on headquarters and working, sometimes hard and sometimes otherwise. McGregor is still here too and the way he's going with a girl he has here it looks as if he'll be married before long. He's beginning to stop on the street and looking at the RINGS. I think when it gets to that stage, it's pretty serious. He's just as nice as ever though... Your Big Brother Arthur"*

A subsequent letter reveals that McGregor eventually was accepted for front line duty. He would later be killed in action on the Russian battlefront. His engagement would never culminate in marriage.

*Jake* was a newer, faddish or *cooler* term meaning okay. If someone was *Jake*, they were on top of the world. Communication to the front lines seemed to also spur community involvement, even through Art. The following is taken from his letters.

*"When I was home on pass in August, I met a little girl by the name of Marianne. Believe me, she's some kid too. She is a schoolteacher and since I got back she wrote to me about three times. She lives south of Lethbridge. When I told her I had a brother overseas, she wanted to know what he looked like and how old he was, and all kinds of questions. I told her that he was a whole lot younger and a lot prettier (and all sorts of lies) – anyway she said not to forget to give you her love. Well now, she's a darn nice kid. I'm enclosing a picture of her and Dorothy Graham. Hope you like it. She gave it to me just for you to see. Well kid, old scout, write often. Your big brother, Arthur.*

*"From Art, October, 10, 1918. Just a few lines, because I'm very awfully busy just now, and besides, I got to go to the dentist to get some teeth fixed (He fix em alright). He pulled out a couple of nerves yesterday, and oh what a nice feeling she was. Say kid I'm all up in the air these days, I got a chance to go to Siberia. At least I think I have, I was up before the doctor to get examined and so was McGregor. They wouldn't pass us at first, but we got a nice letter from the District Paymaster, to give to the doctor and after a while he marked us fit and so I think I'll be going all right. I hope so anyway.*

*"Say kid, remember that girl I was telling you about. I think I sent her picture too – the Manning girl. Well I got a nice letter from her a while ago and she wants me to go to their house for a couple of days sometime and she wrote...*

*"While you'll be here Artie Boy we will write a letter to your brother overseas. I bet he'll be glad to receive some kind of a letter – and do you think he'd answer me if I wrote."*

*"Now what do you think of that? I bet you wish I would go and see her, and I think I will, if I can get off some weekend.…. She lives south of Lethbridge some place. In the meantime we will keep working for the government. Gee its time I was at the dentist so will say gooda bye for this time. Art"*

(From Emile's Aunt Edith, from a series of letters beginning on June 17, 1918.) *"Your father was going to write yesterday evening, but he had to leave right away as he is managing the sawmill right now, and he does not have much time to write... As we all get together as often as possible, your letters are cherished and often composed by all of us together.… They have bought a new saw last week and they will be leaving for Dawson Creek, BC, next week.…. Your Uncle George will be going north at the same time as Uncle Fred and your dad... We pray to God for you,*

24

*that you may have good times and we wish that the Great War will be finished before you arrive at the front lines… There is always news from your Uncle Joe in Madawaska. Uncle George is going north to open the Prince George sawmill, however it is very difficult for him to hire men. All the men available are Indian, Chinese and Hindu. For me, nothing much is new. It is always the same routine. There are not marriages often as the boys are all at the war. Jack Smith that you know through work here was married on Friday and on Sunday evening he left for the Sarcee Army Camp in Calgary. Hope you return in good health to Canada… Uncle George went to the Fair in Calgary, but the Fair is difficult with all the soldiers gone… We salute your courage, Eva sends a hug… Uncle George bought a new Briscoe automobile for $1250.00!… Mselle. Cathrine flew with an aeroplane, but then maybe you have flown often. Charles Ouinette had to marry Leona McPherson, Eva's schoolteacher, in June. Eva is still in school in the Convent in Pincher Creek until the 28th. Hugs, keep strong and great courage, always your aunt. From Aunt Edith"*

One of the letters from Aunt Edith stood out. While most of the letters were of local news, friends being wounded or killed in the war, and as much as possible home-style news of health and weather, the letter of September 22, 1918 was more philosophical.

*"I believe that you are waiting for my letter. I received your last letter and we were very emotional in reading it. You are well and have marched through many areas of the old countries under the flag for Canada. You have now visited France and Belgium. I know it is not the way it should be perhaps as you may now be most often in the trenches, however we hope it is not too terrible and that you remember the good part best. If you continue your engagement of war there, the Germans will evacuate France and Belgium. Their small towns and village lives will be returned to them. It will be a great*

*honour? (n'est-ce pas?) It is very significant with great*
*importance."*

Emile's Aunt Edith then went on to describe Eva's life at
school in the convent and the busy lives of the uncles. The
youngest brother Denise (Jeff) had now quit school and had
joined his working family in Dawson Creek, B.C. and as his
letters were also written to her each two weeks, she went on to
mention the news from the north.

All of the letters from Emile's Aunt Edith were in French,
and were signed with, "Au Revoir ta tante qui t'embrace", or
"Un bon Baiser de ma part", or "bon courage, toujours ta tant,
Edith". She had purposefully taken the nurturing role of mother
to her nieces and nephews, from the day of the death of their
mother, her cousin.

A single letter was from Philomene, Emile's grandmother
and it was dated July 5, 1918. The work of the uncles and the
father was embellished from that stated in the letters of Aunt
Edith. Grandmother Philomene was a very devout Catholic and
she expressed her prayers and wishes for Emile to not forget his
religion while in danger. Her letter was a very candid
communication to an almost unimaginable situation in the
rough trenches of Europe. It was evocative of the reality of this
family being both French and English speaking. Philomene
would not have been able to write in English. The maternal love
given by the grandmother, in lieu of the mother who was now
non-existent within the family circle, was also very genuine and
always in evidence.

The date of November 2, 1918 arrived and with it the
battle for the town of Valencienne. It was one of the final few
last major decisive battles of the war. It also was one where
Canadiansoldiers became known as the strongest and most
fearless group of fighting men- of any force on the Western
Front. Tragically, only one out of five men would not be carried
out by a stretcher or left as dead. During the entirety of World
War I, one man in eleven, who enlisted from Canada, was killed.
In total, sixty thousand Canadians were slaughtered.

* * *

The rain finally slowed to a drizzle. Emile rolled over in the water and mud in what was the remnant of a trench. Bullets and heavy mortar shells flew close by him. With his rifle with bayonet fixed at the ready, held above his head, he is waiting for the next order to charge. Caked in mud, weary to the core, shivering incessantly, he relished these breaks. It seemed that a solid night of sleep with a clean blanket was a luxury found in a distant world. He paused with a thought then and voiced under his breath, to only himself, *God. It's wet, bloody and muddy.* Blood had splattered onto his face from his colleague of the battle who was next to him. His buddy now lay face down, but Emile knew that it didn't matter. The soldier's face had been blown off by mortar fire. Emile eyed him with feelings of empathy, helplessness and sorrow, and he repeated out loud, *God it's wet, bloody and muddy.* Emile knew that he could not reach his comrade to turn him over. He could not manoeuvre through the mud, even if he had attempted to move in the soldier's direction. The mud was thick and deep – he would get stuck. He repeated, almost hollering, *God, it's wet, bloody and muddy.*

Almost two hundred and seventy years earlier, the voice of Guillaume rings out in this French countryside. He had been thrown by his horse and was lying next to a slough. *God it's wet, bloody and muddy.* He had hit his head on a rock and now was wiping the blood off with his muddy hands. *Damn,* he muttered as he slowly rose to summon his horse.

Guillaume is a French name, whose English equivalent is William. The nickname could even be referred to as Bill but somehow this respected name from the past does not lend itself to nicknames.

He is a few kilometers away from Emile's trench. *A few kilometers but two-hundred and seventy years prior.*

Guillaume checked his pockets. He had not dropped anything. It was dusk. He was hurrying through the forest of western France and he was on a mission that would alter the course of his life. Indeed, little did he know that it would affect the next centuries of his entire family lineage.

Guillaume was riding between the home of his youth in the small town of Bresolettes and his new home with his young family in Tourouvre, Perche, France. It was a ride of great importance, he was delivering to his father-in-law a handwritten map that he had finally managed to obtain. It was a sketch of the New World and the land where he wished to take his bride and son. His own father had accepted this fate. As the youngest male, there could be no future in either village for Guillaume. By tradition, the family business would be passed onto his oldest brother. It was a given that he needed to strike out on his own.

His father-in-law, however, needed to see his daughter's destination on a map. Time would reveal that the sketch was really just a guess of the location of the French colony in New France. But for its purpose now, it would keep the family happy. This map was intended to relieve the family's fear of the unknown. Somehow, if they could see him pointing to a destination on paper, Guillaume knew that they would feel better about their departure.

It had seemed that their entire French community was excited about the young couples that were headed for the *New World*. Most of the inhabitants of Bresolettes and Tourouvre were related to those that were leaving.

In fact, it might be said to be a parallel to Emile's Canadian community being excited about his wartime travel to the *old country*. Both parties were equally naive. The proportion of deaths and lives given for the cause; was very similar. The hierarchy of leadership in both periods of history was such that these peasants, farmers and members of the created lower classes were considered nothing but pawns – devoid of human attributes – in a vast political system of power, expansion and corruption.

# Chapter 3 - 1641 Immigration

As he had planned, in time Réne Pelletier had a son, and it was his son Eloi that learned to read and write. Literacy enabled Eloi to be able to achieve the trade of *marchand de charbon,* a coal and charcoal merchant. As Eloi's son, Guillaume would become the third generation to enjoy the beautiful Perche forest - with its small streams and serene lakes - while living and working in Bresolettes.

Guillaume Pelletier had been born in 1598 in Bresolettes to Eloi Pelletier and Francoise Matte. Guillaume felt that, like all fathers of the former century- in this case the 1600's - that Eloi was very strict; however, it was nothing compared with his father-in-law's severity. Eloi was interested in seeing a chart of Guillaume's destination, but he was far less rigid than Francois Mabille.

The Mabille parents had demanded to see a map before they could bless the excursion into such an unknown part of the world. Guillaume knew that his father-in-law M. Francois Mabille likely would be unable to conceptualize distances or directions shown on these symbolic charts. It was simply that he was attempting to assert control over that which he couldn't understand.

As far as Guilaume's own father was concerned, he knew that even though he had fulfilled his consistent duties doing manual chores for his church of St. Pierre in the centre of Bresolettes, his father somehow wasn't satisfied with his achievements. Bresolettes was, and he felt it would always be, a very small town in a Perche Forest clearing. Guillaume was sure that no future of any consequence could ever be found here. He reflected on the concept that even to enter the church, one had to cross through the church's cemetery. Life seemed focused entirely on death somehow. His fellow townspeople seemed in awe of the fact that his church had been rebuilt using a foundation of the remains of an earlier church destroyed during the Hundred Years War. Guillaume wanted a future, not a past.

Tourouvre was on the edge of the forest. Bresolettes was in a central clearing. If for no other reason than to escape temporarily from the claustrophobia of his village, Guillaume had begun to visit Tourouvre whenever he could. Each time that he visited, as he left the Perche forest to walk into the open area of Tourouvre, it was like the opening into another broader world. Even before his marriage there he felt that it was leading to somewhere, out of the darkened shadows of this time in history. He never imagined that it would lead to just that – he could not have conceptualized it leading one third of the way around the world.

## THE MAN OF FRENCH ANTIQUITY

It was said that Eloi Pelletier was a descendant of Barthelémy le Pelletier of Brittany who had been born in the 1300s. It was also said that Eloi had inherited his ancestor's obstinate behavior against the new human freedoms - at least that was Guillaume's perception of his father. Barthelemy le Pelletier had been given a portion of the Perche Forest by the French King, Charles V, as a reward for his bravery in the battle of Thouars, in Poitou, on August 7, 1375. They had triumphed over the English *Black Prince,* one of many marauders, who had been invading the French King's territory and had carried out an atrocious massacre of the civilian population. Barthelemy was considered the local hero for leading the successful fight against the infamous Black Prince. Two hundred years later, the Pelletier family had not forgotten this fact; however, its value was only as local folklore, as the family members were not tempted to live behind a façade of elitism. The reality of life in the aftermath of these battles had removed any benefit. The family no longer owned any of the forest, and liaisons with royalty had not existed for anytime remembered.

When English captains such as the Black Prince fought with their foreign knights and adventurers, they did so for pay and booty. Often their pay stopped following the local horrors of war when their monarch was no longer in need of his hired troops. Edward III was one of the kings who felt no responsibility for seeing that his soldiers returned home after disengagement. They would proceed to live off the countryside, wandering about its farmland and plundering at will. Freed from what little discipline their generals had been able to impose, these men became fiendishly cruel marauders. Attempts had been made to send them off to other lands, but this part of France was good plundering. They were not easily cast off as when the nobles of the region grew desperate and marched against them, these outlaw companies usually won – being very adept at battle.

The peasants of the countryside surrounding Paris suffered desperately from these unsettled conditions. In effect the war had not ended and the government simultaneously demanded heavy taxes for the costs of their most recent large battle. Over and over again the peasants had seen their fields laid to waste and their homes destroyed. The local nobles, humiliated and demoralized, did nothing to stop the brigandage. Rather, they added to the peasants' distress with even more new local tax extractions. When a lord or his castle was captured for ransom, the peasants had to contribute to the ransom. To the French noble it seemed far less trouble to collect the new tax each time than to defend their lands, properties or people adequately in the first place. These uncontrolled companies of men and their offspring were to be the bane of French existence for two centuries.

Throughout this period, the toiling Pelletier family was part of the peasants entrenched in this partial enslavement. Guillaume despised this, as did most able-bodied men, and he was looking forward to a future free of the pronounced cast system of France. At least this was his expectation. Reality would prove that the hierarchy would be almost as formidable in the New World.

In Tourouvre the revival of commerce had begun to play an important part in stimulating the growth of urban life. Many of the people who lived in newly formed villages would still farm in the surrounding countryside or they would pasture animals in the commonly owned fields. They were free individuals except for their liability to the arbitrary taxation.

Guillaume had attempted to mesh his skills with the new industries in this land that could be described as quiet rolling hills. This ancient province of Perche was becoming an important iron-works centre, especially in the nearby Avre River Valley. Its picturesque setting, with small farms of wheat, barley, oats and hay intermingled with dense humid forests, was now undergoing profound change. Guillaume wanted more than what this industry near his hometown could offer. He was like the *Percheron* draft horse bred in his province and already famous. Guillaume also wanted to go into the world as far as the Percheron.

The rural poor scrounged for food and fuel in the forests, marshes, moors, and hedgerows, or in the fields following the workers after harvest. Society was sharply stratified, the social gradations steep. It had nuances that were obeyed and understood. Status affected a peasant's seat in church, and in his position on a Saint's Day. Class lines were formalized with distinct styles of dress, diet, habitation and entertainment; with each having its own training, customs and mental attitudes. In today's world it is difficult to imagine not being able to wear a certain garment because of being in a different class; however at the time, this hierarchy was considered to be a very positive measure of civilization. The contemporary belief was that social hierarchy preserved political and economic order. To believe in the equality of human beings was to be uncivilized.

France often seemed old, tired and too densely populated to each subsequent generation. This was also a time of revolt against all traditional views of biology, chemistry, botany, physiology, astronomy, literature as well as against the ingrained standards and values depicted in art at the level of the educated or informed. All former intellectual authority regarding the classical and medieval thoughts was often times questioned by many Europeans during this period.

The French civil wars of 1562 to 1598 were still a handed down form of memory in this region. After those years of turmoil, Guillaume had been born just at the onset of relative peace. France had been nearly torn apart by forty years of agonizing, destructive civil war. Further religious warfare had begun in the early 1620s in southern France and was still continuing in the form of sporadic revolts.

Guillaume's fall from his horse happened near *La Grand Trappe*, the original Trappist monastery. A neighboring village of Soligny was now being formed as individuals there decided to live in a cluster. He now rode slowly along a winding trail just below the monastery, in order to let both his horse and himself compose themselves. Guillaume reflected on the fact that if he had been more seriously hurt the monks might have offered to help. He wasn't hurt, however, so he rode on, now speeding up again into a cantor.

The Pelletier ancestral home in Bresolettes had solid walls made of flint-stone, and would be renovated and still standing in the twenty-first century. It was half-timbered and of exceptional construction, as were many of these homes in the area that became Normandy. Large hearths were the focal point of every bedroom. Hundreds of visitors later would attempt to envision their ancestor Guilluame and his younger brother Antoine as children playing rambunctiously in the yard. However as Guillaume contemplated his small family's survival and well-being, it was impossible for him to dream that far into the future.

As a *marchand de charbon,* the trade handed down from his father, Guillaume could not have had a more stable income. He usually got paid, although often it was in barter. The town charter of Tourouvre had stated specifically that a merchants' guild could be formed. The guild had secured a monopoly of the town's business for him. Dealing in coal, a resource in great demand, meant that Guillaume had more security than most tradesmen. However, lifting a sack of coal or attempting to carry several of them up to third-floor coal storage creates an understanding of the hardship of this enterprise.

In this area there were many guilds to which artisans and merchants belonged. Ordinarily the merchants within their guilds had the higher income of the two; however, they all struggled for economic survival. Even though the merchant guild had secured a monopoly of the town's business for its members, the individuals who controlled the guild were not above adding their younger relatives to the list of any industry that seemed lucrative. The officers of the guild were the same individuals who were the officials of the town. They operated in the two separate capacities, seeking always to enhance their personal benefits first.

However, high justice and government rights still remained subject to the ultimate authority of the king. As commerce and the exchange-of-goods economy began to create a middle class, or *bourgeoise;* there evolved wide differences, both ideological and practical, between groups and their guilds.

The most important asset to Guillaume and others like him was their freedom. An understatement might be that there was no love lost between these townsmen and the nobles of the countryside. The merchants considered the nobles to be idle men who could and would plunder and tax them whenever the ongoing opportunity arose. Guillaume knew that within this system, as a coal merchant he would never have the opportunity to rise to the level of the wealthy merchants. He would always remain at the level of those who did their own manual labor. As a business owner, he would hire out some of it; however truly reaching the level of the clean-cut and well-dressed bourgeoisie would not be a possibility.

A doctrine of nobility by birth had developed slowly over the previous centuries, and it was clearly intended to keep the townspeople in their place. Nevertheless, a continual, quiet movement from the merchant into the noble class did occur, most often through service to the crown. A naivety would later follow, as on the basis of this premise, young settlers to the New World would identify with serving their *king and country.*

The church regarded commercial activity with suspicion. Since the objective of trade was to make money, and any type of materialism was considered a deadly sin by the Christian morality of the time, the church dictated that small merchant transactions were only fair if there were a minimum of profit. Large-scale commerce seemed exempt, however, it would radically be demonstrated within the system that was to pioneer the massive development of Canada. It was the church, hypocritically, that had consistently reminded the masses that not that much time had passed since the existence of the pure feudal system when the serfs had been bound to their lords. Church leaders expounded piety and gratitude to the former ruling lords for having freed individual serfs.

To obtain their freedom, the former serfs of these newly formed villages sold the surplus they had achieved from hard labor. They then paid their lord ongoing taxes for their freedom. Thus the freed peasants still owed rents and services to their lords, which was now fixed by a charter. In theory, the peasant was no longer subject to his lord's arbitrary will. But consistent unilaterally declared changes in these payments were a part of the peasant's day-to-day drudgery and existence, and would be for years to come.

D'Alexandre de Lavone began his tenure as the seigneur of Tourouvre in 1570. He would make sure that his crest was carved into the St.-Aubin Church, to be found in the town's square. Like all nobility, he felt that this was some assurance of eternity.

* * *

On February 12, 1619, Guillaume had left Bresolettes to marry Michèle Mabille. Born in 1592, she was six years older than he was and possibly because of this age difference, her parents, François Mabille and Etiennette Monhay were excessively controlling. He could never decipher as to whether they had always ordered him about because of the difference in age or because of his age in general. Guillaume would work very hard at his solution to the rut that he found himself in life.

Guillaume would always remember their wedding at the St.-Aubin Church at Tourouvre. The church was magnificent. He had often read its cornerstone. The original date of construction was 1034. He knew that it would probably be standing for *a thousand years* into the future. Above the altar was a fifteenth century painting of the nativity that was placed there to be enjoyed by others in perpetuity.

His bride, Michèle Mabille had been baptized here in 1592. As he reflected upon his nuptials, he had been simply a pawn both during and after the wedding. It had been his in-law's church, their home and their friends. Even though such issues were traditional, he really hoped that the situation regarding his lack of control issues could change now.

* * *

The three great feasts of the church and the lives of its worshipers were Christmas, Easter and Pentecost. These represented the celebration of the birth, the resurrection and the descent of the Holy Spirit fifty days after the resurrection. However, the number of holidays now set aside to honor popular saints had steadily increased to almost one hundred per year.

The cycle of festivals for the farming year began at the end of September after the harvest was gathered in. This celebration was marked by the feast of St. Michael and All Angels with this Michaelmas being the name for the common day for beginning leases, rendering accounts and paying annual dues

Next came the celebration of Halloween, a feast of the dead that was a mixture of paganism and Christianity. This celebration was held with a belief in the presence of the spirits of the dead. In order to ward them off, church bells were rung all night, large bonfires were lit and people danced around them, sometimes disguised in masks.

Surplus animals were slaughtered in November and the meat was salted away for the winter. December was dominated by preparation for the Christmas festivities that began on the 25th, and it was an old feast of the winter solstice. Ever since the fourth century this day had been named as the occasion for the feast of Christ's birth. It was followed by twelve days of holidays, culminating in the feast of the Epiphany on January 6th. This was a time of great celebration and often it allowed for relaxation of normal moral standards.

The later dates of the feasts of the year would also be upheld for several centuries following. In the fashion of fireworks of later centuries, the villagers would celebrate Midsummer, which was also called the feast of John the Baptist. In reality it was a celebration that had remained from pre-Christian centuries. Youths would run through the fields with flaming torches while rolling burning wheels down the nearby hills. This life in early France would be replicated in the lifestyles of the early pioneers of New France.

The seasons of feasting were often followed by seasons of hunger, when one crop had been consumed and the next one not yet gathered. However, there were now some outside sources from nature to draw on. Still, life for the trade and peasant class would remain precarious.

They were still very close to nature. The nature that they knew was of the existing virgin forests and it was then less tamed. The wild animals that now only haunt European nursery tales prowled in their wilderness and could be found even in the cultivated fields. Because there was no lighting in the towns, the nights were darker, and the cold seemed more intense. It was a backdrop of a more primitive time, when people submitted unquestioningly to the uncontrolled forces of nature. This required mental conditioning and a confidence based on faith alone, definite assets when faced with the unknown odds of a very harsh New World.

***

As Guillaume attempted to count the number of families that had discussed moving to New France, he realized that they were over eighty in number. Most would leave from this rural region between 1634 and 1651. Throughout the preparations, he was at once both optimistic and frightened.

Guillaume initially had moved in with his bride to her parents' home, north of Tourouve, called Babonniere. They eventually were able to move out on their own to Gazerie, a cluster of buildings, slightly west, but still to the north of Tourouve. It was the perfect location for them - almost half way to Bresolettes if the path was taken on foot. It most often was, as the cart was kept for hauling coal.

Guillaume and Michèle were close as a couple. They had three children: Claude was baptized on February 11, 1622, Guillaume on February 26, 1624 and Jean on June 12, 1627. Two children died in early infancy, a reality in this harsh life.

Both his innate optimism and the politics of the era would now play an important part of Guillaume's life. In New France, the settlement of Port Royal on the Bay of Fundy had been founded in1604. The first permanent settlement in New France, it was also the oldest on the North American continent north of Florida, but the British would destroy much of it in 1613. Port Royal was then rebuilt by Scottish colonists and it repeatedly changed ownership between the British and the French. In 1713 it was renamed Annapolis Royal.

As if this tug-of-war between nations wasn't enough to discourage any pioneering spirit, there were other divisions among the French. Paradoxically the Catholic territory of New France was a mostly Protestant undertaking. Samuel de Champlain himself is shown to have been Protestant, as his biblical first name seems to suggest. On his first voyage to establish a permanent trading post on the Atlantic coast, a bitter quarrel had broken out between the two denominations. The unhappy legacy of the religious war in France would continue to create bitterness and divisions. For one-and-one-half centuries between 1560 and 1715, Western Europe was in a nearly constant state of war. There were fewer than thirty years of international peace during this time. From 1560 to 1650, the common denominator of war was Protestant and Catholic religious strife.

As a second deterrent, the French investors also adamantly disapproved of the heavy investment of both time and money into colonial settlements, as they considered this to be to the detriment to the fur trade. In France, this battle with creditors for long-term support would be lost.

Since Samuel de Champlain had founded Quebec in 1608, the European population there had grown slowly. Champlain's twenty-eight men who had stayed in Canada over the winter had built the original site of Quebec. They had proven the winters could be endured. In 1617, Louis Hebert and his family, as the first colonists, settled there, and by 1620 the entire European population was a total of sixty. However, the settlement had not yet learned to become self-supporting.

Even as adroit and resourceful as Champlain was, he could not make useful citizens out of a secondary group he referred to as the *dregs*. They had been plucked from the prisons and gutters of Paris often against their will, and in many cases they continued to focus only on their drinking and gambling habits. At most they might hunt and fish sporadically. One of the only skills they acquired in this wilderness was the smoking of fish. They learned this skill from the Mi'kmaq Indians they encountered on the eastern coast, who lived partly off the fish they caught in inshore waters, and which they usually smoked.

In France, Cardinal Armand Jean du Plessis de Richelieu had begun his rise to power in 1616. This was an era that is often referred to as the period of the *Ministériat de Richelieu*. His politics, held in a negative light at the time of his creation of the thirty years war, kept him from initially focusing any attention across the Atlantic to France's colonies. He had gained complete direction over the corrupt court of Louis XIII. These were also the years of the Musketeers, the bodyguard army of the king.

While the king of France showed no interest in New France, fortunately Cardinal Richelieu assumed this responsibility. At the time of signing one of the most significant documents in Canadian history on April 29, 1627, Cardinal Richelieu was powerful as chief of the King's Council. He was able to create and organize the Company of the One Hundred Associates, also to be later known as the New France Company. This company was made up of one hundred investors and its mandate was to own and exploit the vast unknown regions of New France. The monopoly it was given was to last for a minimum of fifteen years. In return, the partners were required to furnish three hundred colonists each year, for fifteen years. As its part of the bargain, the French government was to provide two warships fully equipped for service. The Company was to support each new colonist for three years in return for his labor. Originally the company was to own all of the land and could grant estates called *seigneuries* under existing French feudal laws. The *seigneurs* were to gather about them a community under feudal rule.

Robert Gillard, a pharmacist and an adventurer who had grown up in the Perche region, received one of these grants. Guillaume knew him only by reputation. In 1634, Robert Gillard was named seigneur of the Beauport area, just northeast of what is now Quebec City. His goal was to recruit colonists from his native Perche Province. The Juchereau brothers from the town of Tourouvre were his principal recruiters.

The Juchereau brothers had a signed commitment from Guillaume Pelletier and his bachelor brother, Antoine, before 1640. However, life and death interceded and just prior to leaving, his elderly in-laws became very ill. Guillaume and Michèle were forced by conscience to stay. Both Francois and Etienne Pelletier died within a short time of each other in 1640. The now small Pelletier family was finally free to leave Tourouvre for a new life in Beauport, New France.

# Chapter 4 - Rough Passage

The concept of emigration- leaving one country and becoming a citizen of another - did not exist for the family at this time. The move was perceived simply as relocation to another part of France. They were leaving for New France, and the difference was the promise and the opportunity there - a better life for everyone.

Both Guillaume and Michèle had been worn down by hardships. The death of their parents was now just a reminder of the death of their two sons, one of whom had died in childbirth.

Because of what they had suffered, taking part in the adventure of the New World was much easier than it might have been. A dramatic change was what they needed. Antoine, the quiet brother of Guillaume and his closest friend, above all wanted opportunity. Life in France had offered him none, and so he had happily joined them.

They also were to serve their king, hierarchal masters of state, and their god. At all these levels as they understood them, they were completely trusting. Like all of their peers, the Pelletier family trusted that the individuals making the decisions concerning their fate within this hierarchy were never irresponsible. As being devout men and women, the Pelletiers would serve their superiors and know this was the best they could do – they must always be resigned to their own fate.

Given the excitement for their future, Guillaume found it easy to say goodbye to his relatives in France as did Michèle to hers. It had been much easier than if their parents had still been alive. As well, their land transportation to the seaport had not been as difficult for them as for many others. As a coal merchant they owned a horse and cart sparing the family a long arduous walk on foot. They owned two carts, the larger of which was left behind in Tourouvre. With it they had always been prepared for hard-working days, sometimes into the twilight, with their large and heavy loads of coal. It had a five-foot box, with sides that were also five feet in height, all supported by large eleven-spoke hardwood wheels. Two Percheron draft horses pulled it, harnessed in tandem, in order to effectively pull such a weight. However, for this new journey, Guillaume used their smaller cart and his single horse. This was their older animal - and one that was in need of retirement from the burden of hauling coal.

From Perche to the port of La Rochelle it was an eight-day journey. Just before their departure by sea, Guillaume had traded the horse, the cart and even some coal that he had thrown into the cart for good luck, in exchange for light tools and warmer clothing.

Upon approaching the gang plank to the waiting ship, they would enter another realm. The Pelletier family were not prepared for this ship from another world. As if to accelerate their transition, a small man, speaking in the French language of the sea, made his presence known. "I'll let ye know your directions, me mates!" He was shouting as if they had approached him from a country that did not seem to share his language.

"Me captain tol' me to help ye. Here's how it goes: 'Aft' means towards the stern or rear – right? 'Aloft' refers to anyplace in the masts, yards or rigging. 'Astern' is behind to stern– right? 'Athwartships' is across the boat. 'Below' refers to anyplace under the main deck– right? 'Forward' means towards the bow or front of the vessel. Ye got that?" He bellowed with laughter. These were farmers; he knew they hadn't got it. This was his world, not theirs.

As a deckhand, the small man knew his place, but these moments were his glory. He was in his element; with a chance to boast of his knowledge. Ordinarily a trade ship with cargoes of fish it now carried much more interesting fare. He continued: "'Poop' is a small raised deck near the stern. 'Port Quarter' is on the left, facing forward. 'Quarter Galleries' are small balconies on the after sides extending to the stern. 'Quarter' is the side of the vessel from midships extending to stern. 'Starboard quarter' is on the right, facing forward." Laughing again he set them straight on the location of their cabin. "Just go down over there with your stuff. Ye can stand backup here to watch the land sink away after. Ye'll be standin' over there when ye come back up – out of our way." He laughed again, a likeable chap, despite his crude mannerisms.

Little did Guillaume, Michèle or Jean know that "below decks" was where they would spend most of their time during sail. Upon this discovery, fourteen-year old Jean put on a brave face, almost tempted to volunteer his services on deck. Realizing that he didn't even know the language of sailing, French though it was, he quickly set that thought aside. Michèle simply gazed out to sea and thought about how deep it looked. As for Guillaume, he initially took the practical stance and was attempting to lead them down to their quarters. They had each been given a passenger number, and that determined which bunk they would sleep in.

Over the period of the voyage, many of the farmers onboard would become acquainted with their ship and its strange and new culture. She was of a design called a Caravel. She was a fifteenth and sixteenth-century cargo vessel that displaced about two hundred tons, rigged with three masts and a bowsprit, lateensails with frequently used square sails on the fore masts, along with a spritsail. She was gaff-rigged with a four-sided mainsail. A halyard hoisted and controlled each sail. They were rigged with up to three masts - with a mizzen-mast stepped on the transom with the mizzen sheeted to a boomkin, and also rigged with lateen sails. This allowed sailing close to the wind for efficiency. To many of these former residents of the rural community of Tourouvre, the subculture and language of sailing was distressing. Jean was more positive and immediately accepted it as a sign of things to come, and a promise of a unique future.

The ship was one of the frigates of La Rochelle. For one hundred and fifty years the harbour of La Rochelle, on the west coast of France, was the main point of departure. Nearly all the trade with France would pass through this town. A shorter route for the settlers of New France, known as the *Royal Route* would be used only a few years later. It terminated at the port of Brest.

Michèle's first observation had been that the deck was slippery and soiled with gobs of tobacco juice spit. It was inevitable, as the deckhands had busied themselves hefting bags aboard, reefing lines through blocks, tarring the shrouds and reaming up deadeyes. She assumed this was all logical and she wasn't about to speculate on what was really happening. Later she would realize that fewer than twenty seamen sailed aboard as the usual ship's complement, and in age they ranged from an eleven year old sea-boy to the elder sixty-year old boson-cook. Her second impression was that of complete chaos.

The captain gave orders from the top deck shouting out to the sailing master to haul sheets and get the bark moving. In little time the lusty sea chanties could be heard from forward as the jack-tars went about their practiced duties, shaking out topsails and courses and hoisting a pair of jib sails. As they pulled out into open water, the towline fell off and the sheets *came home* filling up with beautiful wind. With her yards braced on a reach, her topsails, courses and jib sails set and drawing, their small bark heeled a little and then sped along under every inch of canvas she could muster. They would hope to make a good speed, trolling along at six to seven knots per hour.

Even during smooth sailing, a hundred creaks and ticks resounded off the wooden walls, as the ship heaved herself along, the deck knees and ribs working, the foremast step at the very foot of the bulkhead issuing intermittent groans. The captain's demeanor was such that he could provide some assurance of competence to the settlers. He was very formally dressed for the time, in a brocaded long-coat, silken hose and buckled shoes, as was his first mate. The first mate wore the same costume as his master except for its color and its ornamentation, which was calibrated to be a scale lower. They were bareheaded with hair tied in a pigtail with a miniature bow; however the captain would often wear a traditional wig.

As if a subtle warning to the uneasy passengers, the captain could be heard as he shouted to the sailing master to "snug her down good and tight, with hatches battened and all loose gear stowed in good and proper order."

They most often ploughed through the sea in their ever-changing fashion under topsails and two jib sails, heeling as she smashed over the close-ranked waves. Ever so often she lifted her stern to a longer ocean swell running under the keel, barreling up at a rate of knots and setting up a nasty cross sea, like a broken-wheeled cart. Overhead, the topmast groaned at the trestle trees, where they were joined to the lower masts, adding the nagging worry of gear failure to other concerns.

Unless the ship's awkward motion prevented it, the sailors had been busy reaming up the standing rigging, holystoning the deck-boards and scrubbing the main bower cable. It was a distinct air of brisk, well-disciplined determination. Swells would be heaping up to the height of two stories and the bark rolled and yawed contentedly as if this was normal life.

If was normal to the sailors it certainly wasn't to these farmers from Tourouvre. Often too much speed was gained as the ship surfed down the biggest waves' backs. This sinking feeling was dependant on the helmsmen as he simultaneously kept a true course. Lifting high on a swell roaring under her stern she would then smash against the rudder blade as the helmsman struggled against the wheel's kick.

However no matter how weather-hardened even a sailor might be, the blind ruthless passion of the sea beneath a tormenting wind could undermine even his experienced resolve. For the Pelletiers, it was hell. As the timber frames protested and the mast-steps would creak, even the hardened could become very insecure. The uncertainty of the strength of the stem post and the carpenter's scarf joints at the deadwood, misgivings about the knees and frames in the way of the shrouds and channels, and also the plank fixings of the scantlings of the ribs were all a nagging doubt when sailing in the center of this vast ocean. These small ships, not much larger than any boat, needed to take punishment as they harnessed the cold heavy winds of the Atlantic.

It was often as if the bark had been picked up by a giant's hand, to be played with like a toy. From astern, on rushing waves with smooth faces fifteen or twenty feet high, reared up and raced down to catch the little ship, swinging her quarters one way and then the other, like a dog's wagging tail - taking each roller with an uneasy irregular wiggle. The noise was then infernal, like the roar of a landslide, as the top of a wave broke and a hundred tons of sea raced towards them- a curtain of white foam running on its face, barreling down to then explode against the quarters.

Clear sky was necessary for the calculation of latitude however cloud cover could last for days. Preparation for storms was more specific. The sailors would depart to the shrouds and begin their climb up the foremast. Others stood ready to tend the lines on the deck. The helmsman would keep the bark steady with someone staying nearby to call the waves. The captain would often stand by the break to oversee the reefing.

The sailors moved slowly and deliberately up the ratlines. At length, about three would shuffle out along each yard arm, both port and starboard, feeling for the foot ropes as they went. The bark was then swaying fifty to seventy feet from below. These masts yawed and arched across the sky as their hands clawed at the heavy wet canvas with freezing fingers struggling to tie off the reefing pennants while the wind whipped at the lines. A bight of loosened canvas, caught by a gust, could render a man insensible or knock him clean off of the yard arm.

Once they had tamed the foresail with a reef, halving the spread of canvas, the ship rode easier. They could then descend from the foremast to struggle along the heaving deck to mount the main mast and continue reefing there in what seemed an unending battle between men and the wet cold elements.

Looming from the night at anytime an immense wall of water could bear down upon them. They hung on for their lives from all parts of the deck. Tons of freezing water often washed aboard and the individuals were sent tumbling by the torrent like matchsticks. The ship would roll until she stopped falling and steadied as the keel ballast did its work. She would then begin a slow heave to come upright. The masts would whoosh through the air exaggerated by their angle. The settlers would immediately have scrambled down the companionway to below deck- as soon as possible.

Often the outcome was tattered sails streaming in the wind. Lines and reefing pennants thrashed and snaked wildly, smashing blocks and clattering against the masts. Broken yards hung askew and upper ratlines drooped slack and lifeless. Shrouds were frayed to thread with much of the rigging gone. Work was then simply scheduled to refurbish all that was broken. Land had to be reached in some manner.

Their sea-charts were cursory at best. Ahead and to the north lay a vast shore marked on sea-charts only as *Terra Incognita*, with vast lands of either islands or continents of which no one was certain. Dead reckoning was most likely in error by many leagues and they were forced to sight their landmarks near arrival in order to determine their actual fix.

The journey was difficult, as they coped with rotten or unusable food, ill heated conditions, and the appearance of scurvy. After the first few days they had to depend on the food supplies in rancid barrels lashed outside of the galley. The menu consisted of dried eels, salted fish and beef, along with fruits and some spices. When the weather had proven rough, the port lids were closed and the tiny cabins would become dark and cold. For their own safety, the settlers were often temporarily locked in. Many of the colonists became sick and weak, in a condition such that: *the respect to the common wants of nature was not possible to them any longer*. This was accompanied by an inevitable stench.

Hunched up against the sharp wind, they would stagger toward the weather rail, only to be reminded to *protest to the lee side – never to windward.* Here, like a cathedral gargoyle of the same era, they could open their mouths in wide and ghastly yawns and release the putrid stream of juices and pottages from the bottom of their stomachs.

They would often not make it up to the outer deck areas. The between-deck areas were like a dungeon. When the hatchways under which the people were stowed were finally opened, the steam rose and the stench became like that from a pen of pigs. The air would become so foul that they were often driven to the dangerous upper deck, risking the rush of water that still waved across their small ship. The few beds they had were in a dreadful state, for the straw, once wet with seawater, soon rotted.

There were numerous occasions of the *conveyance to the railings*; a deceased body sewed up in canvas, to be committed to the deep. The funeral service was of a special nature. If the winds and waves were calm enough, the foresail was set as being of a *broach to* as an offering to God. In high winds however, this set of the sails could be dangerous. Everyone onboard stood in a double row on the deck, each holding a burning candle. The body was carried along the line accompanied by the priest following it as he chanted. Each individual would touch it as a parting gesture. The priest read the service while often discreetly balancing himself, by standing to the side and holding onto the rail. The deceased was then slid down the plank that had been laid across the ship's railing. The bodies were always buried from the starboard side, as they slipped into a sea that was perceived as being bottomless. It was accepted that some of the semblance of a ceremony could be set aside, when either extra canvas could not be spared or very rough waters disallowed it.

A lookout was scheduled in spells, and the sailors swapped their time throughout the day in order to keep alert. As they closed in on the new continent they were also to look for chunks of blue-gray ice. Some were the size of a small boat and were broken, half-melted floes or pieces knocked off larger icebergs. The smaller pieces could be shrugged aside easily enough, though these pieces battering the foreparts of the hull could be a constant and unwelcome tattoo destroying any possibility of a full night's sleep.

In the New World and around the Gulf of St. Lawrence, the sea-ice cracks in April and loosens in May. It floats free in June; thus the timing of the voyage was critical. As they approached the coast, fog would be expected. Heavy mists could roll down to envelop them in a clammy soup, obscuring everything, the sun, the sea, the sky and the shore. In minutes it could become so thick that, from the quarterdeck, the anchors stowed in their catheads right forward would become invisible. When having to go aloft, the men had developed a system, as they lost sight of each other halfway up the ratlines, in that they worked together by using their shouts and chanties. It would be as if eerie sounds were descending from the silent damp clouds above. Each day it was hoped that the fogbanks would lift by noon.

It was this scenario that reminded the Pelletier family and their new friends that many of their kin back in France truly believed that they were flying in the face of God's will by venturing so far west. They had often heard that this was against nature and was all too likely to "goad the fates" into a fearsome retribution.

They believed that penance alone permitted them to avoid penalties for sins, and this only if they had been truly repentant. The basic idea behind the penitential system of the time was relatively simple. When one was sincerely penitent for sin and confessed to a priest, one was saved in the sense of avoiding hell. However, a stain still remained on the soul that had to be erased by a sojourn in purgatory. This could be shortened or even avoided by doing some act or acts pleasing to God. A practice that had evolved from the Irish had reached France. It was the frequent confessions of all such sins. Even after all of this, it still remained that by possibly flying in the face of God's will, they were not just endangering their lives but also their souls for eternity.

Related to these fears, sea creatures were taken for granted. New types of ocean organisms were found every year. The science of the century dictated that they could be assured that huge monstrous ocean ogres would be rising out of the sea. They simply presumed, not that the monsters did not exist, but that they might be spared in having to confront them. During this period many French painters depicted the mysterious demons and dragons of the deep.

Perched high at the main-topsail, a seaman finally cupped his hands and cried, "Land there!" The leadsman with his line at its fullest stretch of a hundred fathoms, was still reporting with his call of, "No bottom found." However there was finally the call of, "Bottom found, eighty fathoms, small shingle and slate stones."

Salmon was plentiful in the St. Lawrence. As they had sailed into their eastern destination, Indians had come alongside with their daily catch, both smoked and fresh, which they exchanged for biscuits or pork. The fish were caught in wicker baskets shaped upon stakes stuck into the sand within the tidemark. The baskets had two entrances, one pointing up the river, the other pointing down. These usually had no doors but had sharp pointed wands to prevent the fish from exiting as they headed into the basket. The Scottish settlers later observed that the traps with doors were similar to those used in their homeland.

The floats of wood that seemed to resemble small floating islands were already appearing on the great St. Lawrence, as they would glide slowly and majestically down the river past them. These huge rafts were covered with turf and had a wood hut situated in their center, such that they were very different than sea going craft. These bateaus were a flat-bottomed type of riverboat and could be initially seen with their smoke curling up from their roofs with children playing in front of the hut door. The matron often was sitting and sewing while the husband guided his family's craft along the banks with a long pole. Often a dog or two barking added to the unusual perception that this was a town lot with a natural home as it went floating by them. Upon having traded their wood upstream, they would make their way back to their home in the same manner of using the river. In later years these people would mostly settle on land, on the north shore of the St. Lawrence River, as the short summer season consistently hindered annual use of the river. The practice of living this way existed in Europe, however never were the rafts of this size. The narrower European rivers would dictate that a different style of live-aboard barge would evolve.

Quebec was named by its Algonkin name, which means the place where the river narrows and here it did narrow considerably. When the French arrivals had completed their slow navigation up the river, and upon sighting the wharf, they were joined by two launches taking their towlines out bow and stern to keep their craft on station. Their ship was small enough such that it could manage the river, however these lighter and more maneuverable boats had now been designed for river travel. They finally were able to drop their jib sail and let the staysail sheet go free as they jostled alongside the wharf with precision. After a three-month journey, the Pelletier family could now return to the world that they were familiar with. It was the world of farming and related commerce – and it was on land.

Having secured to the wharf, the seamen settled the bark. They then busied themselves with folding the sails, boxing the yards, and coiling down the lines as they always had done. In spite of their travels, the sailors as individuals seemed almost unworldly. They led a largely sheltered life with their domestic and financial arrangements being made for them by those whom they served. Going to sea as a sailor was almost equal to joining a religious order. The traditions of the sea were now including specific prayers to the saints, and this group of devout men was always resigned to their fate and whatever the storms might bring.

The perception of the foul mouthed, drunken irresponsible type may be left for tales of pirates of the Caribbean. As was often the case upon their arrival with having been so long on salt provisions, these sailors would usually drink too much fresh water at once, in the first few hours on shore. This would give them dysentery for up to six weeks until they would again return to the sea. Sadly, they all too often really didn't become acquainted with the exotic shores into which they had traveled.

As the Pelletier family set foot on the shores of Quebec, the entire European based population of New France was now two hundred and forty in total! Their neighboring colonists to the south had landed at Plymouth Rock in 1620, in a ship called the Mayflower. Only 149 years had passed since Christopher Columbus had initially sailed to America. Cabot, the Italian sailing under the English flag, had discovered Labrador in 1497. Their concept of voyaging into the great unknown along with both its presumed and actual risks can be extrapolated from these dates.

Like other new settlers in 1641, the Pelletier Family imagined that they had left risks of torture, death, and famine in France. The risks in the New World, however, proved similar with different players in the same process of survival. The increased risk of torture, death, and famine, were most importantly exceeded by the challenge of the cold winters. They would win and entire New World future generations would be the recipients of their accomplishments.

# Chapter 5 - The New Start

When he and his family left France in the spring of 1641, at forty-three, Guillaume was now a considerable age for both the era and such a profound life change. His wife Michèle was forty-eight. Their son Jean, however, was at the ideal age for such an adventure. He was fourteen.

Antoine, Guillaume's younger brother, had joined them with enthusiasm. They all looked forward to working quietly and diligently for the next three years for "the Company" – the time that was a requirement of passage. Work as carpenters and woodworkers was plentiful and very much needed in this new colony. Having worked in a trade rather than in manual agriculture qualified the three men for jobs working with wood. On occasion they would move between Quebec City and Beauport where they would work directly for Seigneur Robert Giffard.

## THE PIONEER

During the ensuing thirty years some seventy other seigneuries would be granted. Upon the arrival of Guillaume Pelletier and his family, the total French population in the colony, which included settlers, soldiers, clergy and fur trade company employees, numbered only about 240 people, but by 1663 this number would increase to 2,500 people.

Robert Giffard was to prove to be the ideal seigneur by the settler's standards. He had given the first arriving immigrants accommodation with food and clothing if needed; they were then put into the process of helping to build his manor house. Individuals not trained or able in construction were delegated to clear the land of trees or work in sowing the soil and the following year they were able to harvest their first grain. The harvest, however, proved to be not quite enough to subsist on. After two years of clearing the land, many tree stumps still remained. The produce total was eight barrels of wheat, two barrels of peas and three barrels of corn. During this second year, the Pelletiers had arrived.

\* \* \*

Before their three-year contracts expired, the Pelletiers were assiduously laboring at building their own dwellings. By September 12, 1644, Guillaume was proud to become a formal owner of a piece of land in the Seigneury of Beauport. When he acquired the property, it was already an established parcel with a six-acre frontage between the St. Lawrence River and the Montmorency River. It extended northwest to the river and was only one property away from the west of Montmorency Falls. This cataract was eighty-four metres high. It was thirty metres higher than Niagara Falls, and as such it was a splendid natural monument that added to the excitement of their new lives. Antoine was as hard a worker as his brother, and he bought the piece of land between Guillaume's property and this great waterfall.

With this process of property acquisition, the Pelletier family was promoted from the rank of immigrant (colon) to that of free farmer (habitant). This freedom had a levy, however. Each year on an appointed day, the habitant had to pay seigneurial dues or else deliver produce of equal value in kind. These first farm lots or habitations could be inherited, deeded or sold, but not detached from the seigneurial obligations as specified in the title deed. For the Pelletier family, like others, it was easy to rationalize that their habitant society was still much less stratified and dictated to than that of the peasantry in France.

The term habitant therefore must not be confused with paysan or peasant. Habitant is a word borrowed from the West Indies meaning a factor in charge of a colonial enterprise. A difference did exist, however, as the West Indies colonists formed an oligarchy, which possessed seigneuries and controlled the councils that were associated with their governor. In contrast, Guillaume and Antoine Pelletier's group held much less authority. From 1647 on, groups of habitants formed committees with elected local representatives, but political power remained with the seigneur.

On the day of payment of the annual levy at the manor house, the habitants were to show their allegiance and homage to the seigneur. All the habitants would gather amid boisterous festivities for the Planting of the Maypole. On this occasion the seigneur was treated with great showing of loyalty and honor, a local process that was in reality feudal.

Each step of development and every detail of existence was dictated by rules set out in the cabinets of the new autocracy back in France. True free will was denied to the new settlers.

A share of the prosperity of the seigneur, within whose system the Pelletiers worked and lived, was to a certain extent handed down. They lived in reasonable comfort for the time, and were able to provide for the family adequately. Even though Guillame did not own and hold the land by"freehold title" standards, the fixed dues or money due to the seigneur were considered reasonable: the payment was a few bushels of wheat per year. It was judged to be a very fair system superior to that which existed in France, at the time. Ownership of land, as we know it today was neither expected nor discussed.

Milling charges for the seigneurial monopoly were also considered reasonable and consistent. A monopoly dictated that all the habitant's flour must be ground at their seigneur's mill yet paid for as if worked by outside labor.

The seigneur held all of the rights of hunting, fishing and water use. He also controlled the right to erect sawmills. If Guillaume sold the farm, the normal charge of one-twelfth of the value of the land as tax would be due to the seigneur. The first seigneuries were on a tract of land on each side of the St. Lawrence River, an area varying in depth from ten to forty miles.

As habitants, they had now become free to marry at the church in Quebec City. For this first generation of habitants, the marriage contract might well have been signed at Robert Giffard's manor house, as it was the centre of life at the seigneury of Beauport. For the Pelletiers, however, Jean was not yet ready for marriage and Antoine was occupied with other thoughts.

After becoming an established a landowner, Antoine did what he deemed the next logical thing and had Françoise Morin, his long-time sweetheart, move in with him. It would never be documented whether this was a *"marriage à la gaumine"* a process based on a strict interpretation of the Papal ruling that marriage required the church's blessing. Although the concept of Antoine's less formal liaison died out in the eighteenth century, he would have identified strongly with the process. This brief, practical custom showed that some people viewed the church's strict rules as hindrances to logical marriage. "Marriage à la gaumine" held that people who wished to marry without either their parents' consent or without a proper wedding would attend a regular church service and announce at the end of it that they regarded themselves as married. Often they would stand and smile or wave at their friends and family as the priest attended to the mass with his back turned. All would consider this the announcement of alliance. These nuptials, informal as they were, side stepped church attitudes of the time.

One of many examples of unyielding church doctrine was that the priest was expected to remind the newlyweds that: "your wedding bed will someday be your deathbed, from whence your souls will be taken to be sent before God's Tribunal. The bed in which your children are to be conceived and born is not a place for pleasure."

Marriage had been a serious dilemma in the history of this church, and it was recognized as a sacrament to solve the dilemma of recreational sex. The church had consistently preached the superiority of the celibate life in accordance with its abstinent tradition. Yet if all men and women were celibate, the race would quickly disappear. Hence, marriage was regarded as a sacrament to dignify intercourse engaged in with the sole purpose of creating many children.

To these people who believed, as did most Europeans of the time, that the priest changed bread and wine into the flesh and blood of Christ, the mass was a majestic miracle and the true symbol of the spiritual powers of the church. Baptism, confirmation, marriage, birth and death dedicated steps on the path of every Christian. Yet paralleling this piousness were new ways of thinking and a new way of life - particularly for individuals who had been willing to travel in the face of the unknown to cross a ferocious and mysterious ocean. By the very fact of their arrival in the New World, they had proven they would act against deep-rooted tradition.

In general, the new Canadians were very much freethinkers in a world that required, as the twenty-first century expression quips, "thinking out of the box". There wasn't a civil marriage system available as an alternative; indeed, there was no civil status at all. It was a given that such things could only be provided by the church. For this reason Antoine Pelletier identified with the logic of *marriage à la gaumine*; and it was unfortunate that for this very reason his marriage to Françoise Morin could not be considered legal.

Whatever its negligible status or legitimacy, the informal marriage of Antoine Pelletier and Françoise Morin, was short-lived, for two months later on October 3, 1647 Antoine drowned as his canoe overturned near the Montmorency Falls. He was an expert in canoe use and it was not a mysterious death. His farm was only a stone's throw from the upper head of the falls. He would have used the river as transportation. Over-exuberance while imbibing and visiting with friends, along with canoeing home at dark, could easily have been factors. This was the downside of the location of Antoine's farm. Like all commuting, then or in the future, it had its dangers in festive times.

As Antoine and Françoise had not entered into a formal marriage contract, Guillaume now inherited one-half of his brother's land, subsequently buying out Antoine's widow's half of the property. Later, in 1655, Guillaume sold his brother's former property to Jean Migneault. The value of these lands was much less than the later concept of outright farm ownership. The land was a place to live with certain privileges but with an overriding commitment to serve. Guillaume would also become involved as both a community leader and construction manager.

He had become a master carpenter and beam-maker. Having achieved success with this craft, Guillaume was instrumental in the construction of Chateau St-Louis, the governor's home in 1647 and of the parish church in 1648. The Ursuline Sisters in Quebec had made a specific notation of this. If he had ever intended to be documented as a pioneer of Quebec architecture he had decidedly achieved his goal.

Many craftsmen were needed for this new colony, and from 1641 on they had arrived in large numbers. As masters, apprentices and laborers, these workers would soon forget the customs of the motherland and begin to forge new traditions. Some of the traditions were embellished. At the annual processions of the Fête du Saint-Sacrement held in June, each appointed representative marched, carrying a torch, according to the rank of his guild in Old France. In the procession of 1646, there was a carpenter, mason, toolmaker, baker, brewer and sailor. Only two years later, in 1648, there were twelve categories, which included a joiner, carpenter, mason, turner, locksmith, gunsmith, toolmaker, shoemaker, cooper, baker, wheel-right and nail-maker.

Guillaume participated in the *Communauté des Habitants*, the landowners' syndicate, and was elected to represent Beauport within this group in 1653.

At the age of fifty-nine, on Tuesday, November 27, 1657, Guillaume Pelletier died. He was buried the next day in the Côte de la Montagne cemetery at Quebec City.

His wife, Michèle, stayed living at the Beauport farm, where she died eight years later, on January 21, 1665 at the age of seventy- three.

Life had been a partnership with her husband both in raising a family and earning a living. For over five hundred years, it had been a tradition of family and race that the wife of a craftsman, guild member or farmer, would work alongside her husband with equal purpose. Female roles during Michèle's life had included remarkable women– Elizabeth I, Mary Queen of Scots, Catherine de Medici, Louis XIV's Madame de Maintenon, all who exercised considerable power. For the first time in history, a power shift favored female prominence. One-quarter of the Parisians arrested in a political demonstration in 1557 had been women. Female roles were now changing in all spheres. However, a negative counter balance was emerging. More than ever before, "women's work", was becoming the work that men could not or would not undertake.

For the rural population of both Europe and New France, field labor was merely replaced with a new type of domestic drudgery. There was throughout Michèle's lifetime a never-ending schedule of labor. It was true that the ornate dress of an aristocratic lady was a costume that made any physical activity almost impossible. In contrast, the country womans' cap, thick dress and clogs were designed to protect her from dirt and enable her to work simultaneously in rain, cold and mud.

The work of plowing was left to the men but the women helped gather the harvest. Gleaning and picking up grains of corn the harvesters had left behind was commonly the younger women's task. Just as in medieval times when the women had for many years of their lives carried baskets of animal dung to help manure the fields, Michèle Pelletier had looked after the animals the family kept around its house – the hens, pigs and cattle. The spinning of thread was also traditional for older women, hence the word spinster. In her later years she had also cleaned, cooked and baked while lovingly caring for the younger grandchildren.

Michèle was buried beside her husband after an unusually long life as the ultimate pioneer woman and her husband's equal.

The generation of Guillaume and Michèle Pelletier served New France without question of motivation, resources or usury. Life existed in a new form, which to them represented opportunity. However, their son Jean was among the many younger settlers who were jaded and cynical about their government-controlled futures. Before Jean had sailed with his parents under the financing of The One Hundred Associates, other ships had already been sent.

One such group of four hundred passengers never reached their common destination. Becoming a victim of the ongoing hostilities between France and England, their convoy was intercepted by warships led by a notorious group called the Kirk brothers. The Kirks had been born in Dieppe, France, to a French mother and an English father. As Protestants, they had sought refuge in England from the cardinal's persecution. Initially, they had wanted to settle in New France; however, the French cardinal had decided that "heretics" would no longer have the right to immigrate there, and he sent a fleet full of mission- aries to offset any possibility of that happening.

In the earlier part of the seventeenth century, the Kirks were a part of the Calvinist bourgeoisie that was well known by the settlers, as the Kirks had sailed to Quebec and had demanded its surrender. Champlain had lacked food supplies after a winter of holding out, had no choice but to concede. Louis Kirk landed his one hundred and fifty armed men and planted the English flag on one of the bastions. Champlain was then escorted by one of the Kirk brothers to England, where he learned that at the time of his surrender, the war between France and England had been over for three months. Champlain immediately launched a campaign to annul the conquest. The outcome was that Charles I of England agreed to return Canada back to France, on condition that Louis XII pay him a debt in full. This quick decision allowed Champlain to return to New France and rebuild the now devastated Quebec.

To the young Jean Pelletier, knowledge of this futile process gave him an astute perception of the ineptitude of the constantly changing government and its military. It was also apparent that everything political was simply decided by the toss of a coin, or by banter made over wine and bacchanalian feasts. Even important issues relative to Royal Accent and government was by way of either rumor or misrepresentation of fact – all being at best second rate. With an *attitude*, Jean had perhaps shared not just a little in common with the character of his more individualistic uncle, Antoine Pelletier.

In defense of what was becoming the attitude of status quo, the Intendant Jean Talon had communicated the following to the French court, "One must not expect to make people here submissive and always respectful of the King's law and of those who represent his authority, since there has probably never been a country where so many people, even the foremost in every profession, have sought to deny it."

Jean Talon was the most successful of the appointed Intendants. Even though it was the highest appointment in this new land, his vested interests were unique, in that he was neither a soldier, nor a missionary nor an explorer. For the first time, under his direction, the administration of New France would be focused on rural agricultural realities and peaceful lifestyles. In that aspect, Jean Talon was a businessman, within the ultimate industry of agriculture. This did however, consistently include his (people) husbandry schemes, such as "King's Girls" shipments. His popularity may always be that, in all of this, he was very straightforward and never devious in admitting his intent.

Les "couriers des bois", the brash young men of the village who were unwilling to be told what they could or could not do, set out from their communities in increasingly higher numbers. Jean Talon called them "bandits" and the church decrees made them outlaws. However, they opened up the interior and enlarged the fur trade, becoming ultimately, a positive part of the country's creation. Their exodus from the small eastern villages was so great that at one time the loss of the male population from Quebec was estimated to be one quarter of the male population.

The habitants had learned to use the cold to preserve food, and their homes withstood frost and thaws. Their clothes were warm and they learned to adapt to travel on snowshoes. Like those before them, they relied upon produce from their gardens of corn, a patch of barley and an acre of wheat. Wild strawberries were put on slabs of wood and set in the sun to dry. In winter they were taken out and eaten with maple sugar. Roast venison with boiled herbs was followed by a dessert of a pudding of cornflour, lightened with eggs and sweetened also with maple sugar. The venison course was served on many festive holidays. Cloths were woven and dyed bright colors for the women's dresses and scarves. Rushes were often used for mats and bags. Men's suits were made of deerskin. They had indirectly learned local applications from the Micmac Indians by putting balsam gum to use for wounds, red ochre for insect bites and hemlock tea poultices for bruises and sprains.

Life for the settlers of the New World was not all toil and drudgery; some recreation was imported from France. The Pelletier family, like many others, had packed a simple item that provided amusement and that did not require much excess space within their luggage. They had brought their ice skates. There was a second reason for the packing of skates. Simply, they were a sharp utility piece, should the need arise for them to be re-molded into knives or utensils of any kind.

A common theme for the landscape painters of the early seventeenth century were the skaters on their rivers and lakes. Women skated with full skirts flaring out in the wind, and the men dressed up for the occasion.

Jean Pelletier shared the kinship of many as his countrymen held a common birthplace. In the seventeenth century, the province of Perche was part of Normandy and it was the French province from which some of the oldest families of Quebec had originated. Jean would have known the names well. Baril, Beaulac, Bouchard, Boucher, Cloutier, Drouin, Gagnon, Giguère, Lambert, Landry, Leduc, Mercier, Rivard and Tremblay were among the most common.

# Chapter 6 - The Habitant Environment

As the younger and the only surviving son of Guillaume Pelletier and Michèle Mabille Pelletier, Jean became an adult with the handicap of great expectations. He was baptized at St. Aubin de Tourouvre Church on June 12, 1627. The first fourteen years of Jean's life were spent in Tourouvre, France, where he received a relevant education of the time and of France. When he accompanied his parents and his uncle Antoine Pelletier to New France he would not have been of the same mindset as the older group. History has shown the evolution of each generation to be consistent in the one fact: the problems of the time, place and culture will always be tackled uniquely, with all the resources at hand.

In Tourouvre, France, Jean had shown his independence, his determination, and his capability for hard work. Prior to boarding ship, he had shown himself to be a diligent worker in both a sawmill and as a carpenter. He had also helped his father as a coal merchant.

During the span of time from 1641 to 1646 Jean was a young helper in the construction of early important major buildings in Quebec City. After the Pelletier family's purchase of property in 1644, he assisted in cultivating their new farm, as would be expected of all those who lived and worked in this pioneering group.

In August, 1646, at about nineteen years old, Jean became a donne of the Jesuits; that is, he gave his services to the Jesuit missionary cause. In return, the Jesuits promised to pay Jean's family one hundred francs for the first year of his service. Being involved with them would alter Jean's way of thinking even further. The Jesuit superior, Father Jean Lalemant, documented their every achievement in detail and with consistency.

The Jesuits also provided training to young ladies. They called it the science of crafts - *la science des ouvrages* and it was given along with a program of training in which they learned to read, write, play the viola and excel in other fine arts such as embroidery. The goal was two-fold. Not only were the settlers' homes to become fit habitations by the Jesuits perceived standards; their churches also needed embellishing. Public welfare was linked to spiritual salvation and included in it were the Jesuits' general and fine arts programs.

Much change occurred within only three or four years. In 1642, the Jesuit Isaac Jogues was captured and tortured by the Iroquois before being released. He returned in 1645 and, using his newly acquired knowledge of their culture, he quickly committed himself to living among them as an ambassador of peace. In 1646, Isaac Jogues was slain by a single axe stroke from one of the many unconverted Huron.

As if in a surreal feature film scenario of epic proportions, Jean and many other loyal men left Trois-Rivières late in the month of August in 1646. Their fleet comprised of eighty canoes with a single mission. They were bound for *Sainte-Marie-aux-pays-des Hurons*, with each man making a commitment to protect this important fortress. Located on Georgian Bay, the survival of Lake Huron would prove to be pivotal to the history of Canada. At this time, however, the compound included the church, housing for its members and the Jesuit missionaries, workshops, warehouses and a small medical dispensary. Jean Pelletier spent nearly a year there, returning to settle permanently in 1647.

As Jean had joined his contemporaries to work to found a "Christian community for the conversion of the natives" they were aware of their own relevance in history. This was the Jesuit mission statement shared by the settlers and it would not have surprised them that the outpost would be restored much later, with their sacrifices and risk well documented. It was a difficult time, testing each individual's strength of character on physical, mental and emotional levels.

The late 1640s was a time of annihilation of the Huron by the Iroquois. This effectively put an end to the French-Huron alliance. Moreover, approximately one-half the Huron population of Georgian Bay died during this period of various epidemics brought by the Jesuits and the *coureurs des bois*.

Only a few thousand Huron survived. When Champlain had visited Huronia, just a few years prior in 1615, he counted thirty thousand people living in eighteen small towns. Even though it was not recognized as such by either France or England Champlain found a complex and well-organized civilization. Having learned survival skills from the native Indians, the local settlers had come to acknowledge and respect their civilization as a part and parcel of their new country. Unfortunately this overview was too little, too late.

Throughout the seventeenth century, the Iroquois were a military force to be reckoned with. The twelve thousand members of the Five Nations could summon twenty-two hundred disciplined warriors at a moment's notice. Ten percent of the European based population was killed in Iroquois raids. Not only had the Iroquois seized control of the fur trade, they had created a situation whereby it was dangerous for the French Canadians to go hunting or fishing without fearing for their lives.

The settlers no longer focused on further clearing of the land. They felt that the expense of bringing horses from France would be wasted; the Iroquois would simply kill them upon their arrival. They also recognized that France was not interested in helping with military support – its attention was engaged in a war with Spain.

The liaisons between the Indian Nations were dissimilar; however, they were important to survival. The military alliance of the French with the Huron had slowly led to permanent ties between them. Because of the traditional enmity between the Iroquois and the Huron, the Iroquois consequently remained enemies of the French. The Iroquois Confederacy consisted of five nations, the Mohawk, the Seneca, the Cayuga, the Onondaga and the Oneida. The Mohawk nation had been originally in conflict with the French on the St. Lawrence, yet after 1660 the missionaries resettled the now sedentary Mohawk peoples close to Montreal. The community of the Pelletier family would continue to live in relative harmony with the Mohawks until the end of the French regime.

When Jean Pelletier returned to Beauport and the comforts of his parents' home, he was twenty-years old. He was ready to focus on both civilization and family.

## THE ARTIST

French Canadian architecture and wood carving was on the edge of rising to great artistry. The style and decoration of the churches and public buildings followed the taste of the seventeenth century of the motherland. The schools of arts and crafts of which Jean had taken part, were based upon an agricultural community where young men learned to read and write, as well as devoting much of their time to handicrafts such as joinery, lock making, painting, pottery, woodcarving and tailoring. It was through these years that Jean first became known as *the goblet maker*. He excelled in the making of ceramics. Advanced students in letters or tailoring also had learned crafts as a diversion from their usual work. As such, he could both teach and learn; in both cases he was escaping from the normal life of hard labor. Being involved as one of a working force with the Jesuits was also a great honor and one of faith for this member of the Pelletier family.

Like other craftsmen of early French Canada Jean was an artist in the context that the mere assemblage of boards or general material did not satisfy him. He had a natural urge to embellish his pieces, giving them a character of joy and harmony. From the poorest non-land-owning peasant, to the wealthiest seigneur, things of beauty were of prime importance. It was often written that in this period good taste knew no social barrier.

In the latter part of Jean's century, thanks to the efforts of the Intendant Jean Talon, as well as the infamous Bishop Laval, the philosophy of being devoted to educational pursuits evolved into two formal schools of arts and crafts in the colony. The subjects now included science that being navigation and seamanship, sculpting, carving, paneling, carpentry and joinery, architecture, silversmith work, and pottery. Exquisite furniture, beautiful churches and ornate chapels were becoming a part of their community. However, the isolation from France that was to follow would prove to be a cultural disaster. The break was so complete that the heritage of this evolving *school of design* later fell into oblivion.

Pottery is a primitive craft being mixtures of workable clays, which become permanently rigid by heating. In both Tourouvre and Quebec, clay was available and its plastic nature lent itself to a great variety of forms. Late French medieval pottery was restricted largely to serving pitchers, jugs, and cooking vessels, most of which were unglazed until after the ninth century. By the twelfth century, glaze was more often used to create a waterproof coating, but it was generally confined to the insides of pots and goblets. Rough and porous in texture, they were grit-tempered by the addition of quartz sand or ground shell. Glazes were based on lead oxide, and after the twelfth-century, copper was often added to provide a green colour, or iron for yellow.

French medieval potters glazed their pots by brushing them with powdered galena gum that they made themselves - which is highly poisonous. Many died and attributed the cause of their sickness incorrectly to alcoholic poisoning. This was not a process of knowing the mineral composition; rather it was a learned experience of knowing which rocks could be ground to make the desired substance. This more basic process Guillaume had learned from his father. In growing up in the large village and creative centre of Chartres, René had observed imported pottery technique. Jean had learned a refinement of this process with the incorporation of slip evolving from his one year with the Jesuits as a donne. It was training held in high regard at their school of The Science Of Crafts. In this he could excel beyond the former successes in clay of both his father and grandfather.

Kilns needed no complex system and were built at Jean's first two habitations. He created an excavation into the side of a hill giving natural insulation, which, being in a raised position, allowed fuel to burn and provided room for the ash to fall clear for the air to pass under the fuel to assist combustion. The firing procedure was a trained knack, handed down through three generations. When clay is heated above five hundred degrees centigrade, steam is driven off, leaving the clay rigid. At eleven hundred degrees centigrade the mature clay particles melt into one another. Red clay was common in peasant pottery, and the high concentration of iron oxide - as shown by its colour -lowered the melting point of clay. As a known *gobloteux*, Jean would fire the gray clays to a darker and creamier colour. The natural colour is purposely caused by rotten vegetation and was used for high-fired pottery– called stoneware, as well as earthenware.

Jean had been well trained by his father Guillaume. They dug their own clay, which they then purified by breaking it up to remove impurities by sieving. There followed a period of drying, conditioning and adjusting the clay to make it suitable for their handiwork and successful firing. The knack of twisting and kneading the blocks of clay was an acquired experience, handed down from father to son.

One method was that of throwing clay on a primitive wheel; however, due to the size and shape of most cups or goblets, a wheel was not always necessary. The finishing and decorating could have unique and varying thickness, shapes and textures, by way of scoring, carving and beating actions.

A slip, which is a creamy liquid formed by adding further water to a slurry- which in turn is produced by steeping dry clay in water for the casting process – was not a decorative process normally used in New France; however, as indicated by the nickname, Jean Pelletier may have often produced the exception. Slip coating sometimes transforms the familiar appearance of common red clay for aesthetic reasons. However, early French settlers like Jean did not usually use this system, preferring to travel any distance that was required to obtain white clay.

Up to the seventeenth century, the potter sold his wares in his own district. They were simple and unaffected, serving many daily domestic uses: bowls, dishes, tygs, jugs, candlesticks and jars. In this era Jean Pelletier lived and worked with his clay, in a time prior to *English and Dutch Delft Ware and Wedgwood* – and over one hundred years before. European porcelain would be seen in Canada. He would make special pieces in honour of a birthday or similar event and decorate them enthusiastically.

Jean's preference for goblets had to do with both his talent and his specialization. Both as a potter and as a designer he would later be well known, to the extent of being registered on his title of right to farm the land on Île d'Orleans, as "Le Gobloteux".

Fragments would later be found of buff earthenware bowls, with the interior decorated with lines, circles or spots of brown slip, all over a white base slip. Many had a greenish over-glaze. They would survive through to the twenty-first century. These all had unglazed exteriors. Earthenware can be simple, even rough in shape when it is intended for practical use, but when it is intended for religious purposes it can be more ambitious and more aesthetically satisfying..

Jean's goblets were of various designs and uses. They were known as a *brandy-glass, a chalice, a Paris goblet, a quaich, a rummer, a tass or a wine glass*. If one could be located and identified as an earthenware beer stein it would be considered typical. The great museums of the world display examples of these. *Gobelet XIV century, XV century and XVI century* are shown in combinations of silver and gold, purple and white marble and are all on display in the Louvre, in Paris, France. Jean's were not of any exotic material and as such did not survive the centuries. None of Jean's specific work with cups, mugs or goblets would ever be found

\* \* \*

During Jean's life, the "King's Rules" of the day were specific, with the age of marriage being ordered. The parents were to see to it that their sons were married by the time they were twenty and their daughters by the age of sixteen. Any father who failed to do so was hauled into the court every six months until a mate could be found for the unwed offspring. In the event that the bachelors were not coupled, they were not allowed to fish, hunt or trap, or otherwise enjoy the woods. Further they were taxed and prevented from trading with the Indians for as long as they remained in this unmarried state. It was a time of accepted restrictions upon every facet of one's life.

Gradually the "King's Rules" were expanded. Women had to be home by 9:00 p.m.; unmarried girls were permitted to dance only with one another, only in their homes, and with their mothers always present. Rouge was forbidden.

Public meetings to discuss politics were also not allowed. The punishment for profanity was harsh: the man's lips were seared with a red-hot iron. Creativity in swearing was therefore the order of the day with entire books later listing the mostly theological references made to the church and its architecture with an underlying sarcasm.

Jean Pelletier married Anne Langlois on November 9, 1649 in Beauport, Quebec. They had registered their marriage at Quebec City. Most marriages were held in November, January or February, the idle months of the year between the hard labour of autumn and spring. Weddings were one of the main social events of the community, with celebrations lasting several days or even weeks. The Pelletier weddings were not an exception.

In June and July of 1647, the bans of marriage were published three times at Quebec; they stated the intent between Jean Pelletier and Anne Langlois, daughter of Noel Langlois and Francoise Garnier. The fact of three announcements was usual for a traditional family. The reality was, however, that this marriage was a compromise of both logic and contemplation of the probability of these two people being compatible. The parents were convinced that their projections were ideal. Jean was not adverse to the choice. She was a pretty young girl; he could only believe that she would become a beautiful young woman. Anne, on the other hand, had no choice. She was simply told what she should think. *Love would come later.*

The Garniers, one of the maternal families, were neighbours at Beauport. The wedding did not take place for another two years after the published bans, due to the fact that Anne was only ten years old in the summer of 1647. The church would not allow the marriage of anyone under the age of twelve. The wedding ceremony finally took place at Beauport, in the Seigneur Giffard's manor home on November 9, 1649. Jean, age twenty-two, and Anne, age twelve, wed without a formal notarized marriage contract. By having published his bans of marriage when he was twenty, Jean had succeeded in abiding by the 'King's Rules". He had also gained a very pretty bride in the bargain.

The popular bounty called "The King's Gift" went to both contracting parties after they were married within the stipulated age. Although Anne's age was thought to be ideal, Jean was over age by one year, according to the rule for this formal blessing of payment. In spite of this, in later years this gift was be given by the Intendant who became the official who could administer the bounty. He gave it retroactive, as if it had been an oversight.

Bonus payments were an added offering for families, for producing a greater number of babies than had been expected previously. Having achieved ten children, a pension was paid of three hundred livres per year. With twelve, the parents were paid four hundred livres annually.

The young Pelletier couple moved in with the groom's parents rather than with the bride's family, which was unusual for the times. In addition to the parents the Langlois house was home to eight children. The Pelletier homestead, on the other hand, would have only Jean, Anne, and his parents.

Jean Pelletier was also relieved to not take the chance of marrying one of the *imported group of unknowns*, called "The King's Girls" (Filles duRoy"). These were the hundreds of girls sent out from France over a period of two decades to provide the unmarried men with wives. Many were very poor and the king had provided them with a small dowry. Most were about fourteen years old. Upon their arrival at the docks in the harbour, they were immediately paraded about on the wharf for the taking; the unmarried men would quickly choose a fiancée from the chaos of the assembled group.

Girls were permitted to turn down a suitor, but most were not too choosy, as they had accepted their fate and their meager future in the colony. They were aware that once married the laws were specific. The most onerous was not that they were chattels, but that they were expected to be subject to discipline. A separation could only be obtained if their husband resorted to beating them with a stick thicker than his wrist. This was societies only calibration of physical abuse.

However, the more established settlers often envied the King's Girls and their new spouses. Each couple was given an ox and a cow, two pigs, a pair of chickens, two barrels of salted meat and eleven crowns. Depending on circumstance, this could be considered a very good start in life. In the second year of the program, the King's Girls produced approximately seven hundred births in the colony. These were listed in documents, not unlike the production of wheat or the husbandry of cattle, with the administration thus being able to calculate their success.

As these women were chosen for marriage much like slaves at an auction, it was this quick decision process that Jean had feared not only for himself but also for his friends. It was a process that was like the flip of a coin, as it could provide either happy or very unhappy situations that would last an entire lifetime. With its lack of humanism, it fit perfectly within the overall feudal system that was still paramount. However, it also solved the problem of the population being two-thirds male. To the European hierarchy, this type of husbandry was logical to both animals and settlers as a single faction.

Throughout the French regime, land settlement was concentrated in the St. Lawrence Valley from a point a few miles west of Montreal to a little below Quebec, with pockets of settlement on both sides lower down the river. Prior to 1663, the number of settlers and the amount of land cleared grew slowly. The St. Lawrence dictated the pattern of settlement in another way. It was the main means of communication and transportation in the colony - in summer by canoe or sailing barque, in winter by sleigh on the ice. The need for roads was thus not addressed until the eighteenth century. Every settler desired land on the river, and the land holdings almost immediately took on the peculiar pattern that has endured of narrow strips running back from the river. Survey lines separating seigneuries ran at right angles to the river and, as the generations began to hand down land parcels to more than one of the older sons, the individual holdings became subdivided and increasingly narrow.

This pattern of land settlement was not without other disadvantages. Until the end of the seventeenth century, the Iroquois were an almost constant menace, and with the homes separated from one another, mutual aid in times of attack was almost impossible. Individual farms and their occupants could be entirely eradicated before aid could be mustered. While the Iroquois assaults were at their height, fortified stockades had to be built where the people could take refuge with their livestock. This then exposed the vacated open fields of the seigneuries, as simultaneously they abandoned their homes to the depredations of the enemy. However, attempts by some of the royal officials to have the settlers live in villages with their concessions radiating out like spokes of a wheel, in a European fashion. were not successful, even though it provided safety. The preferred world of river frontage, living apart, being lords of their own small domains was coupled with the lifestyle of having access to the wider world that this river access allowed.

The atmosphere of the day was one of an ongoing war, due to this shadow of Iroquois hostility hanging over the colony. The warriors of the Five Nations of Indians had held a large powwow at Lake St. Pierre, and had declared war on the French Canadians. During their first years in the New World the Iroquois had remained relatively quiet. Although it was always felt that they were hiding behind the logs and trees surveying habitant life, few uprisings occurred, so the settlers conducted life as usual.

From the friendly Huron Indians, the habitants had now acquired the habit of smoking tobacco. The Huron grew the crop at various locations along the St. Lawrence River. Despite great opposition from the local authorities in New France, the Pelletier family and others began to cultivate tobacco themselves. It would be later, after 1735, that the colonists would receive moral support from France for this crop. A tremendous demand for tobacco would then evolve.

Several hundred Huron, as refugees from the Iroquois attacks, had settled on Île d'Orleans in the 1650s. Their former population had been estimated at thirty thousand people. Measles, smallpox, and slaughter by the Iroquois had brought their massive number down to this small band. Still, they were not sheltered completely. In June of 1661, the Iroquois captured eight settlers at Beaupre near the original Pelletier farm. Seven more were taken from l'Ile d'Orleans. The settlers were all later killed.

Louis XIV had assumed control of the throne of France in 1661 and the spirit of his times was epitomized by his creation of the court of Versailles in France. It was a complete manifestation of his quest for perfect Roman art and the ideal architectural forms of antiquity at the time. As such, no lifestyle could have been further removed from the realities of life in Canada. Unfortunately, these two very different worlds would stay joined.

Before 1661, the word colony had never been used in its current political definition. Even though Cardinal Richelieu was preoccupied with French domain abroad, he never considered the reality of colonization. Richelieu had taken control over, "the navigation and commerce of France" until his death in 1642. It was always assumed that the interest of the colony must first be the interest of the mother country.

In summary, Cardinal Richelieu appeared to be a best friend of the settlers of New France; news of his death was mourned deeply. In fact, the opposite was true. His primary interest had been in the aggressive growth and prosperity of the colony, but he had established a firm control through the Crown and its ministers, not in any way related to the settlers and their needs or wishes. As Cardinal Richelieu had created this state, nothing to follow could change it; as such it could only fail. However, history would show, that his successor, whose attitude was one of complete indifference, was to be an even greater threat.

In 1663, The Company of One Hundred Associates was dissolved. The now affronted investors in The Company had come to realize that a monopoly on the fur trade was a losing proposition. Many men of extremely poor qualifications had been sent out to govern New France, and had become miserable failures. As another attempt to rule, the Sovereign Council of New France was established. It was made up of a bishop, a governor, and an intendant. The European based population of New France was now twenty-five hundred, of whom eight hundred were settled in Quebec. This total population was a large shortfall from the original goal of The Company, that being four thousand colonists within its first fifteen years. The Pelletier family and their friends did, however, provide the basis and the core of what would become the Canada of the next four centuries.

In December of 1663, Jean and two of his brothers-in-law purchased land on the Île d'Orleans. Jean decided not to move his family to the new home until after his mother's death in 1665. His mother-in-law, Francois Garnier also died in 1665 as a result of an accident. The family ties were lessened by death, and they were now free to move. Jean's new property on Île d'Orleans had approximately a two-acre frontage on the St.

Lawrence River and extended back to the middle of the island. The slope of the terrain meant that the north bank would remain in view. The river was iced-in during winter allowing access, and they could cross by boat almost six months of the year. It would be in this community that Jean would become better known and respected as the "Goblet Maker". In an age where such passions were both respected and appreciated, his nickname, which would survive the centuries, was a hallmark of a new civilization. They located in what is now the western portion of a then newly formed St. Pierre parish on the northern side of the island. Jean and his family remained on Île d'Orleans for only two years before moving to what they perceived as an even better opportunity.

The first overseas shipment of horses had arrived in Quebec in July 1665. There were twelve in number. The enthusiasm generated by the arrival of these steeds was great, but for Jean it was merely an excuse for a boisterous local party. The prevailing view was that the colonies were not, in fact, being ignored as a part of this small attempt at industrial expansion with horsepower; however, for individual habitants such as Jean, the gesture remained singularly elitist. He knew it was a given that he would not receive one.

In that same year, Jean and his brother-in-law, René Chevalier, had purchased a small parcel of land along the St. Lawrence River just below the high cliffs of the upper city of Quebec. The parcel measured only thirty feet by thirty feet. Jean was an artist and he really would have preferred to live in Quebec, create ceramics, and market them from a home that was more commercial. The purpose for the purchase was never documented and there would never be any indication that the parcel was ever put to commercial use. It had been a fleeting dream of his; history and life is like that. The commercial property was sold in 1674 to a man by the name of Louis Levasseur. Jean's dream of commercial artistry was now finally set aside completely.

After his father's death in 1657, Jean inherited his father's half of the family homestead. This was customary under communal property laws. His mother later logically gave up her half to her only son so that now, in 1665, Jean began to rent out this part of his land, giving rights to two acres of frontage to Guillaume Lizot. Later he followed by renting out more land to Guillaume Lizot and Robert Gallien. Jean wanted freedom from the constraints of the rural system and his attempts were now well documented.

Also in 1665 the King sent out twelve hundred experienced troops who had just returned from a victorious campaign against the Ottoman Turks in the warmth of the Mediterranean region. They were presented as the ultimate protection for the colony. However the king's interest in New France was short-lived and by the time the troops arrived they were very poorly outfitted.

Considering the climate from which they had come, Canada may not have been their forte. Nevertheless, they immediately set out with both discipline and military enthusiasm to conquer the Iroquois. During this first attempt against the Iroquois, they soon began to wander, becoming completely lost in the great forest. They were expecting to make a surprise attack on a village but the attempt failed because their guides had frozen to death along the way. Throughout this chaos, four hundred men froze to death while marching. The men were inadequately dressed, almost barefoot and as an ultimate error of judgment they were provided with no pots in which to cook lard to make the traditional life-sustaining soup. They did not have snowshoes, very few axes, no fishhooks, and each had only one pair of moccasins with one single pair of socks. Winter survival in this unforgiving climate would have been near to impossible.

As a further insult, the Iroquois troops that they had been intent on fighting just simply went about their daily lives and ignored them. The Indian band was not impressed by the fact that these soldiers had traveled one-third of the way around the world from Turkey, in order to offer them this feeble challenge.

Finally, French troops of considerable number did arrive. In 1666 a second and far more ambitious incursion was launched. Significantly, six hundred local Canadian militiamen plus a hundred native allies joined the six hundred French troops. They set fire to five large Iroquois villages. With this first glimpse of the new and more powerful military strength, the chiefs of the Five Nations decided to begin the process of peace treaties.

In this initial evolution of a country, an entirely new spirit of expansion and rapid change would evolve, not just here with Jean Pelletier and his family, but also around the world. The census provided interesting details of this society. The population had now grown to 3,418 inhabitants, of whom 1600 lived in the towns of Quebec, Trois Rivières and Montreal. Almost one hundred were parish priests, regular clergy and nuns.

This was the year when the Pelletier family gathered with their many friends, in the community of Quebec, for what was to be "a great market". People came on foot, in canoes, and by ox-carts. Each settler was given cattle, sheep or in some rare cases, horses, by Jean Talon, the Intendant of the time. They were asked to trade their labour in return. This new Intendant presided over the only big wave of immigration in the colony's history. Under the direct authority of King Louis XIV, Talon reorganized the administration and supported the growth of agriculture and industry.

In autumn of 1666, after the crops were harvested and the winter firewood was cut, the Pelletier family returned to Quebec to help build a cargo vessel. In the spring of 1667 it was completed. The proposition had been successful and the ship sailed to the West Indies, laden with staves, planks, cod, salmon, and fish oil. With the return of the vessel laden with sugar for these farmers, New France had established itself as a trading region.

The 1667 census reports that Jean's property had five acres cleared and that the family had a hired hand living with them, seventeen-year-old Guillaume Lemieux. Jean and Anne had nine children. The seven born at Beauport were Noel, Anne, René, Antoine, Jean, Charles and Marie-Charlotte. Two children were born during the family's stay on the island. They were Marie-Delphine, who died four weeks after her birth, and Marie. The ages of deaths of these hardy individuals, no matter how historic, will always mirror the challenges of life. Those that survived to adulthood died at twenty-five, forty, fifty-three and fifty-eight years of age. Given the circumstance, these variances were inevitable.

Prior to the small trading venture with the West Indies, maple trees had been the only source of sugar for the Pelletier family. Each spring the sap began to run freely. The community had previously learned from the Huron how to tap the maple trees by cutting a diagonal incision in the trunk. In the lower end of this incision, they placed a concave piece of bark, which piped the sap into a hollowed log. After the sap was gathered, it was boiled in a large kettle over an open fire. The maple sugar was formed into cakes for later use. Two French Canadian recipes were maple sugar pie, which is a custard-like dish of maple syrup thickened with a cornstarch, and secondly maple syrup dumplings.

On December 28, 1667, Jean sold his first property along with the two adjoining properties he acquired on Île d'Orleans to his neighbour and brother-in-law, Jean Langlois, for seventy-five pounds and one suit of clothes. For Jean, bartering for the suit held with it a consolation that the Seigneur could not lay claim to a fractional ownership of a suit. Île d'Orleans was a beautiful Island, and would remain that way. However, it still was an island, with all of the negative situations living on an isolated island creates.

By the spring of 1668, Jean and his family had returned to the original homestead at Beauport, the lease with M. Lisot and M. Gallien having expired. Son Charles was born on September 25[h] in 1671 at the Beauport home. Being a third generation in this wild land did not hamper the feelings for these roots of the original home. He was second youngest of the nine children and Emile Pelletier's ancestor.

Just two years after his return to Beauport in 1670, Jean became embroiled in a series of court battles over property boundaries between himself and his two neighbours to the east. Theirs was the land closer to Montmorency Falls and the surrounding cliffs of the falls. Both had previously purchased land from Jean, and the original dispute was between these two only. However, Jean became involved because of his previous land sales. This was unregistered land as related to what would later be known as a registered provincial land title.

Court decisions were then made, appealed, counter-appealed, and the bitter process dragged on for six years until 1676. Jean was eager to have all the disputes settled as soon as possible, since he was focused on moving from the Beauport homestead. He then sold the remainder of his father's original land to Charles Cadieu-de-Courville. He was able to finalize the sale in 1676, immediately after the final decisions were handed down on the land controversies in his favour.

Shortly after Jean's life time, the land in dispute, which abutted what is now the center landmass of the Montmorency Falls Historic Site and Park, could be considered one of the most unique properties in all of Quebec. To Jean, it was a property significant only for its nostalgia of family life. Aside from that he considered it poor farmland.

During this period, Jean's wife Anne, at the age of thirty-three, finally received the sacrament of confirmation to the church. She had hesitated for specific reasons. The church could control them a fact of which she was aware. Being controlled wasn't as much of an issue as was whether that control was based on intelligent decisions. Jean and Anne held common opinions in this questioning of the church's intelligent control. They were habitants; they were not scholars; however, they were aware that something was wrong with the system. They didn't have a solution. Pioneering with freehold land was not available to them and church was not separated from government.

In 1672, a new opportunity arose. Jean Pelletier and Pierre Grosleau were asked by Nicolas Juchereau to visit Grand-Anse to evaluate the property of Juchereau's deceased son-in-law, Francois Pallet. The trip represented a major excursion for them. Among other things, they were able to view a better soil. The trip to the new area was enough to convince Jean that it was time to move elsewhere - yet again. He was still seeking a better way.

Two years later in 1675, Jean left Beauport alone to travel downriver to Île-aux-Oies, and it became his tentative choice, but without settling there he abruptly changed his mind. The conditions could have changed throughout the year, or so could the levies discussed with *the Lord of the Manor*. In 1676, Jean settled permanently on Île-aux-Grues with his wife Anne and the five youngest children. In this period of history, it was unusual to move repeatedly; however, to Jean's mindset he was only serving on rented property. Farming at the time, in that place, was a system of usury, and not all individuals could relate to it. The two eldest children, Noel and Anne, were no longer living at home: Anne had been married since 1670 and Noel since 1674. Both were living with their spouses in the Grande-Anse area nearby. Jean and his family then moved in just three years. Not even on the picturesque Île-aux-Grues could Jean adjust to this system of the servitude. He was a man of strong opinions about freedom, and he was a man who created. In short he was an artist. He would have preferred to simply create his beautiful goblets.

In 1679, Jean sold his property to Guillaume Lemieux, the family's former hired hand at Île d'Orleans. Lemieux had now become Jean's brother-in-law, as he had married Jean's wife's younger sister, Elisabeth Langlois Coté, widow of Louis Coté. She had three children by her first marriage and by Jean's reckoning the farm would be their perfect marriage present. It was a sale of convenience to both parties.

# Chapter 7 - The South Bank

Jean and the remainder of his family made what was to be his final move, to the Grande-Anse area. This area included what would become the villages of: Rivière-Quelle, St.-Anne-de-la-Grande-Anse, and St.-Roch-des-Aulnaies.

This whole south bank territory had been ceded to Nicolas Juchereau as Seigneur. Jean and his family acquired their parcel of land at Les Aulnaies in the virgin forest. It had a five-acre frontage on the St. Lawrence River. Being gently sloped, it showed a rich black soil that joined onto the field of rocks slightly below. The river had eroded the boulders into large flat stepping stones, running from their farm into the flowing waters. This area of the river bank was known for a consistent morning fog, but for farming it could be both accessed and used easily.

According to the 1681 census, two years after Jean's arrival he had cleared five acres of his land, and as material gain, he had a total of nine horned animals and a rifle. He was prospering by most standards.

For fifteen years, the area remained as remote as pioneering along this vast river could allow. The Jean Pelletier and the Pierre St. Pierre families were the only two families within many miles. After the chaos and the embitterment of political struggles on the north shore, this was a quiet time of enjoying family, in both Jean and Anne's lives.

On the north shore, the community of Lachine, along the shore of Lake St. Louis, very near their former home in Beauport, was not unlike the community of Les Aulnaies. The seventy-seven settlers and their families who occupied their peaceful white washed houses, with traditional high-peaked roofs; were also hard working with the same proven results from their labor. However, on the night of August 4, 1689, fifteen hundred Iroquois warriors attacked the village. This was a massacre of the worst kind imaginable. Many descriptions of the bloody catastrophe would later be written and they all would concur. The people of Lachine while being devout, kindly and industrious, had set themselves up as victims for this terrible night of torture. It became known as the Iroquois Revenge. That black cloud of fear that had dominated their lives for many years was now shown not to be unfounded. Jean and his family could not help but be relieved that they were at least now living across the river. The river was not a complete barrier; but it increased the distance from the north shore massacre. They could focus on life in their more peaceful community.

As the last decade of Jean's century concluded, other habitants joined the Jean Pelletier and the Pierre St. Pierre families and the concept of community settlement was pursued and even as more families moved in on the south bank, there was a sense of safety and the retention of the enjoyment of nature in its everlasting peaceful form.

As they began to settle, each habitant built a level and sometimes winding road crossing their farm. With the completion of a joined road system, carrying produce by oxen and cart to the seigneur's mill was a much less arduous task. It was just downriver from each new log home, but now it became a safer short haul away.

As life evolved, the children left the homestead, except for Charles, who remained with his parents at Les Aulnaies. His station within the family came with the knowledge that he would inherit the property and carry on.

Jean Pelletier died quietly on February 24, 1698 at St.-Roch-des-Aulnaies, Quebec, at the age of seventy, and was buried at the nearest cemetery at Rivière-Quelle. Jean was buried in March, as the weather finally cleared, after the end of three weeks of bitter cold and blizzard. Waiting out the winter had always been a way of life, and of death. They simply endured it submissively.

Jean's wife Anne moved in with her eldest son, Noel, at St.-Anne-de-la-Pocatière, Quebec, in September of 1700, two and a half years after her husband's death. On March 16, 1704, Anne Langlois died at the age of sixty at La Pacatiere and was buried beside her husband Jean at Rivière-Quelle. During

Jean's lifetime, their descendants grew to include twenty-six grandchildren and three great grandchildren.

In this period, the life expectancy of a woman who had borne over six children was below forty-five years. Anne Langlois had accepted her perceived responsibility of being a part of creating a new population as other women of New France had. They did it with pleasure and pride. It was a pride of self that could only be compared with the dedication of men going forth in battle. Whether logical or not, the same perceived cause of community betterment, stability for the country, and church intellectual superiority was dominant. These perceptions were based on a form of emotional prejudice that can exist only after a lifetime of consistent indoctrination. The church could easily create and maintain this line of thought as status quo in most individuals of this time and place. No one questioned the loss of many female lives that ended after less than forty-five years.

Jean himself had accepted the challenge of the New World but had battled the system to some degree in striving for new thought and a newer system of freedoms. However, not a lot had been accomplished relative to written law or change in his status as a habitant. Information from the consistent system of census would show that he did not die well off. His life was not a stable life, and he did not carry the expected devotion to the soil, which would have been more normal in his day. He cherished both nature and the arts, and in that there is honour. His life history differs little from that of other first and second generation settlers in New France as they dedicated themselves to survival and individuality– along with having to work within an arrangement that dictated their subservient status.

Generations to follow him did benefit from his work, even without the potential for his personal gain within the system founded on usury. Without this structure as it carried on, it may always be argued that there could not have been the evolution of the early communities and the country of Canada as we know it today. For that reason alone, his life story may always be viewed as positive and a valued contribution to the history of Canada.

Three hundred years later, on October 28, 1998, Denis Pelletier, president of the *Association des Familles Pelletier Inc.*, unveiled a monument and plaque in St.-Roch-des-Aulnaies, Québec. It was in honor of Jean Pelletier and his family being one of the first of two families to settle in the Grand-Anse area. It is situated at the Seigneury Mill site and museum, down river from his farm. It is a fitting monument from this century where equality of mankind is the norm. A comparison may be made that in Western Canada the sweat that poured from the brows of ancestors was from their own toil; they were the landowners. In contrast, within the New France feudal system, the pioneering sweat was both for and from that of a created caste system.

In 1679, Jean Pelletier and Pierre St. Pierre had been the first settlers in the area of New France on land granted to them by Nicolas Juchereau. As if to overcome the antiquated system of land ownership, Jean's descendants would own ome of the original land granted to Jean Pelletier three hundred years later. Jean had cleared it and improved it for their use. They would later own it with a form of freehold title.

## THE PATERNAL PARENT

Jean's half of the property was inherited by all of his children, but was taken over by his youngest son Charles, as they expected. It was Charles who emulated his father's love of this farm and this place. They both grew to believe that this was their utopia. Often choices of marriage and therefore community dictated the move for younger men. On January 12, 1704, Charles had bought his mother's share of the property. Charles then worked towards being able to buy out the remaining portions from his brothers and sisters. He achieved his goal.

The first marriage of Charles was to Terèse Quellet on January 7, 1698 at Rivière-Quelle and they enjoyed what seemed like a great life. Their marriage ceremony had provided, no doubt left about their main duty as a couple. Immediately after the officiating priest had blessed the couple, the marriage bed was blessed with the sprinkling of holy water, prayers and exorcisms. The exorcisms were intended to ward off the evil effects of an especially dangerous curse that some enemy of the couple might have put on the marriage to make it barren. This curse was known as the "*nouage de l'aiguillette*", and on occasion the church would dissolve a marriage that produced no children on the grounds that this evil magic had in fact made it barren. Charles and Terèse produced four children together and as a retribution for having a small family, their time was often devoted to helping neighbors who focused on the procreation of children.

As with most families of the time, their lives were very much centered on the relation of family to land. Their farm had to be fertile enough to provide enough to feed and clothe the family. The family, in turn, had to be large enough, and possess enough skill and solidarity to run the farmand to keep it free of debt with meeting Seigneurial obligations. If the family was not large enough or capable enough, the farm of every subsequent generation would be endangered by an accumulating debt. It had become a necessary function of the family to scatter its members, leaving one son behind to inherit the land, and to sire the next generation of farmers.

The following generation would again scatter, while praying for family solidarity with indivisible ties. Jean Pelletier had to carefully distinguish this inheritance among his children and if things did not go according to plan; he would bear the heavy burden of guilt. He would, of necessity express propitious behavior to his inheriting sons. The non-inheriting would feel the burden of renunciation and react with signs of resentment. As in each Pelletier generation, time would be the healer of such things. The indivisible ties have endured.

Such was Charles' first marriage. Terèse died and he married again - and had fourteen children in total. The second marriage was to Marie-Barbe St. Pierre on January 12, 1711 at Rivière-Quelle, Quebec. Only six years would elapse between the births in the two families. Even with two marriages, Charles had been a single adult for less than five years. He had lived up to the expectations of his time and place in history. If the husbandry of this time seems applicable to both man and animal, it is not coincidental. Charles knew that he was expected to be a *stud*, no less and no more than a good horse.

But it was also a communal life and as such it was a happy time. Bread was baked in large outdoor ovens, le fours Turgeon which were shared by several families. In these they also baked beans and tourtières. Their individual wood-burning ovens were made of hard packed clay and stones. Wooden roofs over the ovens kept rain or snow at bay. Masonry root cellars, embedded in steep slopes, were used for winter storage of vegetables.

Between Christmas and Ash Wednesday, each family would make the rounds of the neighbourhood. They danced and sang and thoroughly enjoyed listening to the roving professional story tellers. These free young men seemed worldly, if not sophisticated. Often being from the larger centres of France, they had recently arrived in the colony. *Hospitality was the law of every hearth.* The most frequent of the houseguests was the priest, who carried the rather dated gossip of both the neighbourhood and of the colony. The toil was hard for Charles Pelletier and his family, but friendship and family life compensated. The achievement of work, together with the community of friendship, was an important part of family existence.

Other actions in the New World were taking place simultaneous to the simpler habitant world of Charles and Marie-Barbe. Their king had envisioned French Catholic unity and had entered the Jesuit and Jansenist fray in 1709, by promulgating a papal order that the clergy sign a statement condemning Jansenism. By this order, the seventy nuns at Port Royal were effectively ex-communicated, since it was that particular belief they had studied. The king had feared Port Royal would become a Jansenist shrine, and in 1709 he closed Port Royal and had the nunnery burned. Louis XIV was a Jesuit; however, through these years, both the majority in France and in New France remained Jansenist. The non- conforming but hard-working nuns of Port Royal were seen as a threat to French unity. In fact, this final action of destroying homes was seen by people such as the Pelletier families, as an assault against French Canadians by their king.

This overview is often used in referring to early Canadian history, but the taking of sides between Jesuit and Jansenist doctrines was not the real issue. In the early 1600's, Jansen, a Flemish leader, had changed his name to the more Latin version of "Cornelius Jansenius" and in doing so, he had focused on creating a Roman Catholic reform movement (known as Jansenism). This attempt to produce a revival of the existing theology was done without the approval of the Holy See the ruling body then in Paris. It also contradicted demands of the Catholic faith for a consistent hierarchy. With some of its doctrines, Jansenism was related to the beliefs of the Protestant Reformation. It would now be abolished in the New World by order of the king. As news of the burning was finally circulated, philosophies were never seen the same by the habitants. Hard labour seemed destroyed, and the burning of homes were of a different nature, from the points of view of the habitants of their king.

Like most, the local church on the south bank focused on preaching sermons about the evils of local dances and entertainment. However, society in general knew how to enjoy life without worrying excessively about the strictures coming from the church. There existed a dual track in life, and in love. History will not always reveal all of the formality and rigid rules of the church and of the military. *Normal life* is often shown affected by those rules. In 1716, Quebec authorities had decreed that fast sledding or racing with carriages would be forbidden in the streets with a penalty of payment. In 1713, a ruling banned people from gathering for the purpose of making snowballs and throwing them at passers-by, or even at each other. For the family of Charles Pelletier, it was a pleasant era, but it was also a time of expected rigid behavior. For this they were happy to have moved away, to the much freer south bank.

From 1689 to 1713, the colonies in the northwest Atlantic area were caught in the turmoil of more than twenty years of continuous warfare between France and England. An extravagant and corrupt privileged class controlled the economic system of France. The colonists were not unhappy with disassociating themselves from it. A hard-working class of people in France referred to as the Third Estate supported the ruling class. This Second Estate class – fifteen percent of the population- was dependent on a major tax on the land of the other eighty-five percent of these people.

In France there were also numerous indirect taxes, paid to a designated tax farmer, who was very creative in initiating a variety of added taxes. A tithe was paid, which was that part of their crops and cattle yield that a peasant had to hand over to the clergy of the church. This clergy was referred to as the First Estate and was made up exclusively of a newly established nobility of the robe. These newly established noblemen were not parish priests such as in New France or in a more modern world. They were entirely elite in the true sense.

* * *

Charles Pelletier died at seventy-seven years old on December 30, 1748 at St.-Roch-des- Aulnaies. In his time, the south bank had become established as the new home of the original pioneers of southern Quebec and their hundreds of offspring. Charles had ten children with Marie-Barbe, with Pierre of the noted family line, being the youngest.

The boundaries of Quebec had not yet been defined, and the young men of the day would travel a few miles from their actual homes, thus exploring other villages in looking for where "the girls were." Needless to say, this was a style of single life that would never change over the centuries. It was that which, along with the impracticality of dividing inherited property, had produced much movement of people from one community to another. The Pelletier young men were about to become scattered.

The population was young. The average age was 20.6 years old, 22.2 for men and 18.2 for women. In the area where Charles and Marie- Barbe lived, it was even lower. The average man was 21.7 years old, and the average woman was an adolescent of 16.8 years old. Over half the population consisted of teenagers.

Compared with New England, with its 436,000 inhabitants, New France still seemed like a colony in its infancy, with just 28,000 people. Population growth came from births alone, as there was now little immigration. To the far south, the Spanish empire was now more developed than either the French or British colonies of North America. Interestingly, in Quebec, by 1700, everyone was calling themselves Canadian, and as a group they were in fact, bigoted, jealous and set apart from those they referred to as the Frenchmen.

## THE FARMER

Pierre Pelletier was born February 21, 1731 at St.-Roch-des-Aulnaies and the second Pelletier generation born on the south bank. Pierre married Marie-Madeleine Lebel on June 27, 1757 at St.-Louis-de-Kamouraska, Quebec. Marie-Madeleine had been born in 1734, and she died at the age of thirty-nine, with the birth of Germain in1773. The arithmetic was interesting. She had given birth to twelve children in sixteen years. Among other symptoms, she definitely died from exhaustion. Giving her life for unfounded beliefs or giving her life for her country would not have been considered. She unfortunately died simply doing what was expected of her. As with most women's existence related to childbirth, there was no glory. Their lives could only be made up of as many stolen moments of happiness as they could muster.

As the youngest child, Pierre had no vested interest in the farm at St.-Roch-des-Aulnaies. As a family lineage, the Pelletier family was gradually moving in a specific easterly direction with each generation. Following the marriage in 1757, Pierre would happily move to the home of Marie- Madeleine Lebel of Kamouraska. Two years later, in 1759, local war became a part of their lives. All that they had built, they would now lose. All that the Lebel family had accumulated would be decimated.

British soldiers had moved through the south bank intent on burning all the buildings within the territory. It was a needless destruction of civilian buildings and farms, which was somehow logical to the theories of warfare of the time. The south bank population had not considered themselves to be a part of any war. Their focus was on crops, with the reality of battles being only rumors. Their crops, seed and most livestock were also lost. Surviving the winter, they then regrouped with their community– and together they rebuilt the community of Kamouraska.

They toiled hard for almost one-half a century, they paid their dues to the seigneury and they supported their church and country. In that there is no magnificence. As people of that epoch, they always believed that the fruits of their labour were to be found in heaven. Pierre was buried at St. Louis Church, Kamouraska at age seventy, in1801.

There were really only two classes of people in New France: that of the ruling elite of administrators, clergy and noble seigneurs, and the great mass of working people. This social division was to survive tenaciously in Quebec, and its existence set Quebec apart from the rest of North America, whose greatest strength lay in the dominant middle class.

In France, tax to the monarchy of Louis XV was now increased to one-twentieth of all income. Many tax exemptions were being abolished. Further taxes were imposed called feudal dues and were now paid to the former *lord of the manor*. Since these taxes were brought about simply by searching the archives of records of dues from the middle ages they were always an unknown quantity. They were often arbitrarily doubled due to a new search being undertaken by the tax farmer. Further expansion of farmland in France that would have allowed economic survival also was not possible, as the aristocracy owned approximately thirty per cent of all of the land in France. As these many taxes increased beyond all possibility of payment, many French families lost their land completely. This type of news would be consistently verbally reported, as the newly itinerate farmers immigrated to New France.

The outcome of the French Revolution would be for the former Third Estate, the new ruling body, to call for abolition of tithes and all other feudal privileges. The entire apparatus of feudalism in France was about to be destroyed. However, corrupt government and expensive wars were still to be a part of France for the next two generations. For Pierre Pelletier, New France was in comparison to France, an ideal and preferred setting in which to raise family and enjoy his life and culture. This comparison was often made by way of rumor and conjecture, as far as the habitants having all of the actual facts. Among the rumors and general discussions, they always respected the final choices of their forefathers in choosing this country first.

The wars by the French that had begun in 1740 and lasted until 1763 were also disastrous for French finances. In the year of 1759, the English General Wolfe captured Quebec from the French General Montcalm, at the battle on the Plains of Abraham. This was followed by a regime of military rule being set up. In 1763, Canada and its dependencies were ceded to the British. It is from this period on that the Pelletier family members were, in fact, loyal British subjects.

In the same year, by the Treaty of Paris, France ceded New France to England. It was the British who now faced the difficult task of formulating a policy to govern a colony whose population was different in language, culture and religion from their own.

The global war between Britain and France was of little consequence to the habitants. Communication was poor and the needs of settlers in their humble homes were not political. In centres like Quebec, the British troops paid for goods in badly needed metal coin money, which was a well-known asset. At the point of discharge from the army, the French troops tended to stay behind their battalions returning to France, as they married into the communities.

Of the nine thousand Europeans who settled in the St. Lawrence Valley before 1760, only 350 were not from France. Marriage certificates indicated the parish of origin. Other sources such as marriage contracts, confirmation lists, indenture contracts and death certificates provided additional information, so that the origin of an immigrant and marital status could be easily determined. Their extended community was from France but they remained content to be part of a New France. Unlike the settlers of the first hundred years, in the time of Guillaume and Jean Pelletier, these newer settlers never considered wanting a detailed replication of their former country or their former government.

It was in this new period that the first two governors of Quebec, James Murray and Guy Carlton, both sided with the French-speaking leaders against the aggressive, English-speaking merchants in the colony. Governor Carlton recommended the reinstatement of French civil law, the seigneurial system of holding land, and the right of the Roman Catholic Church to collect a tithe. London, England accepted his proposals by the Quebec act of 1774, and thus completely reversed its earlier policies of 1763.

Just a few miles away to the south, a number of their neighbours would not prove to be as loyal to the British Crown. 1775 was the outbreak of the American Revolution. Their struggle lasted until 1783, resulting in the formation of the United States of America.

In 1789, Alexander Mackenzie made a momentous voyage to the Arctic Ocean. He had discovered the mighty river system that bears his name and he had blazed the first overland trail through the Peace River Country region. This would become a future region of growth for one family of the descendents of Pierre and Marie-Madeleine Pelletier, one hundred and forty years later. Mackenzie's expedition had comprised of ten men: two Scots, six French-Canadians, and two Indians. In the exploration of Canada, the history of great men, great cities and dynamic royalty was overshadowed by the basics of survival. In Canada, not a great French Revolution, but the skills of earlier peoples such as explorers were of the uppermost importance. These were the details of endurance for Mackenzie. Survival could only be achieved with knowledge of details such as the mending of his canoes using a bark patch sewn onto the hull, along with a melted pitch material. In manner, in this wild land, training gleaned from the earlier settlements was paramount.

In 1791, King George signed a bill dividing the colony of Quebec into Lower Canada and Upper Canada. It was considered an impossibility to accommodate the French and the English speaking groups politically. If the two bodies differing in their prejudices, religions, and cultural interest were to be consolidated into one legislative body, dissensions and animosities would surely prevail. It was therefore logical to create two districts with two separate cultures, two systems of law and land tenure, each with their own elected assembly.

In the last part of the seventeen hundreds, the population of French Canada was also defining its taste in architecture. Churches, colleges and monasteries had become the centre of Canadian culture. The churches as places of worship were made attractive and as such were highly embellished. High altars with elaborate ornamental choir reredos were prevalent. Art in architecture was as essential as it had been in medieval times and during the Renaissance. Art was not considered a mere luxury, and it was displayed with the vitality found in early French- Canadian churches. This was an exciting time for art and culture, yet it was a time when most of North America still remained a wilderness.

# THE MEDIEVAL TRADITIONALIST

Jean-Baptiste Pelletier, the second-youngest son of the twelve children of Pierre Pelletier, proved to be unusually traditional and compliant with his own family and cultural environment. In 1791, Jean- Baptiste was elected to a newly formed county administration that now existed due to the new division of Upper and Lower Canada. In 1792, he built a chapel at St.-Roch- des-Aulnaies. He was among many of Pelletier generations who would build churches for their families and for their communities. Uniquely for the time, however, the church built by Jean- Baptiste was named "Saint- Louis", in honour of the king of France. It was never clear why this chapel was erected. It may have been an act of simple piety or that of community spirit. The fact was that numerous churches already existed on the St. Lawrence banks. The new church was not built in Jean-Baptiste's hometown of Kamouraska, but rather in his grandparent's village. In this lies the key to both the reason for building the church and its name. He was attempting to make a positive statement relative to past history and a prior generation. The final outcome of the French Revolution was yet to be determined. If it had been known it would have made the naming of the church more obvious as a misplaced social comment.

The old French custom of church culture as paramount to family and community life, had still survived among the Pelletier clans in their comparative isolation. Communication in the late eighteenth century left much to be desired. People in the smaller village areas would hear about the politics of France many months after events had occurred. Even in France itself, individuals throughout the country would not discover the significant aspects of the Revolution until months after the fact. Even so, the naming of the church at St.-Roch-des-Aulnaies represented an unfounded loyalty to the king of France and the continuing struggles. The vote in the French National Assembly to "taking the king's head" was very close, but the general population of France was no longer royalist. Louis XVI was executed January 18, 1793. Jean-Baptiste Pelletier's dedication of the church to the king (in the year prior) suggests that he was completely out of contact with news of a real nature. If this was not the case, it can be surmised that this church dedication was specifically a family commitment to a grandfather and his beliefs.

In France the great and bloody French Revolution lasted from 1789 until 1794. The rise and fall of several European dynasties had not affected habitant life in any direct manner. In Europe, throughout the Baroque period of 1600 to 1700, as the demand of individual stature was for stateliness and dignity, the elite moved about as if they were taking part in a magnificent theatrical performance. During the Rococo period that spanned 1700 to 1790, nobles dressed as if they were participating in a perpetual operetta – charming, light and frivolous. The shallow French value system of the time, catering only to aristocrats and royalty had no part in war or pioneering.

In New France, some of the neighbouring colonists had been former serfs or statute- labourers and would have no right to land. They lived in abysmal poverty in France. The philosophy that followed the French Revolution with its newly ennobled bourgeois families also was not a part of habitant life. During this period of the French Revolution and a transition in European philosophy, more realistic events relevant to immigrants were transpiring in Canada. Being under the control of a seigneur or a governor did not seem much of a problem to Jean-Baptiste Pelletier when weighed against the proposition of dealing with these greater inequities abroad. To him it was a time of contentment.

Certain French reactions in France were pertinent to the Quebec region. In 1789, by way of the Constituent National Assembly of France and its Legislative Assembly, the onerous yoke of landlordism and feudal privileges and dues was abolished. The entire municipal system and seigneurial system were also being transformed throughout Europe. Through the existing seigneurial system as accepted by

Jean-Baptiste Pelletier and his colleagues, feudal concepts would exist in Canada for another half century.

Jean Pelletier, the grandfather, had inadvertently passed down other biased opinions about the political subtleties of his lifetime. His son, also named Jean, was Jean-Baptiste's uncle. Throughout his life, Jean-Baptiste had heard the story repeated of his uncle's heroics at Rivière-Quèlle in the summer of 1690. It was there that General Phips and his entire fleet met with a standoff from those locally called "the brave defenders". General Phips had sailed up the St. Lawrence River from Boston to attack Quebec City. His strategy was to send raiding parties ashore to terrorize the French settlements along the south bank. To his surprise, the settlers from the Grand-Anse area had been forewarned and were thus prepared. They were able to repel General Phips' raid on Riviere-Quèlle, killing many of Phips' raiders. At twenty-seven, Jean was one of the listed defenders, and the victory lived on as a triumph for his leadership.

Jean senior, the father and grandfather, was sixty-two years old; as the family patriarch, he had put these heroics on a pedestal. Sibling rivalry or family rivalry can be subtle at times. Jean-Baptiste had always longed for a means to compete with his uncle's heroics. By building the church in the name of the king, Jean-Baptiste had gained unspoken points with older generations of the family. By his actions, he had shown his family what he was capable of. The church had been built with emotional prejudice and not specific logic.

In catering to his grandfather's wishes, thoughts and dreams, Jean-Baptiste was reflecting the medieval. An ideal medieval gentleman had many virtues. Through the hierarchy in which he existed, he was to be loyal to his feudal obligations and conscientious in the administration of justice. He was generous, particularly in bequeathing land and money to the church. He was sincerely religious, respectful of church and authority, and faithful to his duties in these. He seldom violated an oath or solemn promise, believing that these were recorded in heaven and breaching them would be divinely punished as perjury. He did not expect change. Above all, he was never disobedient. This was the medieval mindset of Jean-Baptiste Pelletier.

The antique medieval society was sharply stratified with steep social gradations. It had nuances to which all classes conformed without question. Status affected the seat in church, and in his position on a Saint's Day; Class lines were formalized with distinct styles of dress, diet, habitation and entertainment, each having its own training, customs and mental attitudes. Hierarchy was considered a very positive measure of civilization. The contemporary belief was that social hierarchy preserved political and economic order. To believe in the equality of human beings, to the medieval traditionalist, was to be uncivilized.

Jean-Baptiste Pelletier would be the last of the Pelletier family to accept living and working within these medieval social concepts. Within five years, the chapel was renamed, Chapelle Notre-Dame- de-Lourdes. It might be said that Jean-Baptiste was therefore also happy to be part of evolving contemporary thought, as he partook in the ceremony for renaming the church.

Jean-Baptiste Pelletier's life spanned the years from 1768 to 1825. He had a loving and full marriage with Madeleine Pellerin. The marriage took place on October 8, 1793 at that specific new church in St.-Roch-des-Aulnaies, Quebec. Célestin was the third youngest of their eight children. Jean-Baptiste's wife Madeleine would die, as many other female servants of the era, and he would move on in life. Second marriages were the norm and often the solution to raising the children.

Jean-Baptiste Pelletier married Judith St.-Pierre-dit-Desssein on June 6, 1814 at St. Louis- de-Kamouraska, Quebec. They considered Kamouraska to be their family's new home. The older offspring remained at St.-Roch-des-Aulnaies, which was upriver and not a great distance. Aside from now being a settlement where half of the Pelletier family would be living, it was also perceived as the community where their recent ancestors had lived.

Jean-Baptiste and Judith were both in their late forties with existing families to raise. As such, it was generally accepted that they would produce no further increase in population.

As early as 1674, Frontenac, as governor of New France, had conceded this seigneury called Kamouraska. It was eleven kilometers by seven and one half kilometers. When Jean Baptiste's family had moved there, the total population was comprised of thirty families. Just two years after the Pelletier family had settled here, in 1759, British soldiers moved though and had burned all the civilian buildings and farms. Although it was devastating, one hundred and thirty families stayed together, regrouping courageously to rebuild Kamouraska. By 1813, the seigneury had a population of fifty-five hundred. This made Kamouraska a center of both commerce and social life on the south bank. But it also made economic survival on the now subdivided small plots of land very difficult.

It was significant that Jean-Baptiste's generation would be the last of the Pelletier family to live and die in Quebec. Contrary to his personal belief, rival kings and quarrelling governors had not cared nor had they actually done anything of value for the settlers. The Pelletier family owed their survival to their own fecundity and to the often primitive, self-sufficient simplicity in which they lived. Fishing and fur trading had little or no interest for them as individuals as they were hard-working farmers.

## THE REBEL PHILOSOPHER

Célestin Pelletier married Justine Aubut on July 10, 1826 at St.-Louis-de-Kamouraska, Quebec. Two conflicts between he and his father Jean-Baptiste had been prevalent throughout their relationship. In this family, Célestinand two of his brothers were the first to focus on occupations elsewhere. Having chosen to be a blacksmith, Célestin was not entirely out of favour with his father; however this still had represented a choice very removed from the farming tradition.

Since the turn of the century, the port of Quebec, in trading in squared timber, had tripled the number of ships anchored in its harbour to over twelve hundred in any given year. In about thirty-five years, Montreal had tripled its population to over fifty thousand people. Within the context of these massive shifts and the excitement they engendered, Célestin knew it was time to change from serving as a habitant to leading a different life elsewhere. His two older brothers shared in his enthusiasm.

Unfortunately, the family tradition of serving was still his father's guiding principle. There would always be the lingering thought of remaining on the land that both his father and his grandfather had worked so hard to cultivate in Kamouraska in the 1760s. His father had been a teenager during that period, and Célestin was certain that his *younger memory* had embellished the stories of the rebuilding and the ensuing community growth. He didn't mind the stories; they were enjoyable. A father's communication to his son can be like that. What Célestin didn't want was to live in the past. The stories weren't his personal stories.

Being a blacksmith was an honourable trade, and it was essential for the era. Horses needed to be shod and harnesses were needed, and in the early 1800s few other occupations could have been more sought after. Beyond the choice of a new career, the second conflict was one of family settlement and community. Célestin would not have chosen to move to another area while his father was alive. He was a young man and was the sixth generation of his lineage of the Pelletier family to live in what is now the province of Quebec. It was only now after his father's death that he felt confident in starting a new life for both himself and his family. He would move to where commerce and community were thriving in a more free society. Having saved earnings from working as a blacksmith, he was also determined that he should be the first Pelletier to own a farm with a freehold land title.

In this period and in the contemplated move, the first of the contemporary cultural changes were subtly making an appearance. It is the fate of a minority people, no matter what the political system under which it lives, to have changes introduced and flaunted by the cultural aliens of a larger group. This latter alien group, which comprised both the English-and French-speaking population of the growing cities, looked upon the divergent farmers as merely the not-yet-adjusted. The south bank minority and - specifically by Célestin's estimation- the French-Canadians in Kamouraska - all seemed to be defending an archaic order of things, and were not willing to make changes necessary to progress. However, unlike the military conquest of the eighteenth century, ongoing commercial invasions from the main centers that had begun, would greatly upset the equilibrium of the rural classes.

It was no coincidence that his father, Jean- Baptiste, had just died in 1825 when Célestin began planning his move in detail. In effect, it would be just over one year after the funeral that the young Pelletier family would finally leave a feudal system of life. To Célestin it seemed a conclusion to the quest of Guillaume Pelletier, as he had set out with his small family almost two hundred years earlier in search of a freer life. In 1827 Célestin was anxiously looking further east to what would become the Province of New Brunswick. Land, just over the divide of the southeasterly natural water flow, on the beautiful and tranquil St. John River, looked ideal to him.

# CHAPTER 8 - NEW BRUNSWICK

During the first half of the nineteenth century, there had been a considerable decrease in traditional religious observance throughout the entire area of Lower Canada. One-third of Montreal parishioners no longer took part in communion, leaving out even the tradition of Easter. Behavior became so raucous that the legislative assembly even had to intervene in order to prevent congregations from drinking and talking during the mass. This *disrespect* called the authority of the church into question. As an action it was not meant to philosophically reflect negatively or positively on any division between church and state. Clearly people felt that the church had dominated thoughts and actions long enough and began to rebel. The new communities in New Brunswick would be built on a very different foundation of thought than the attitudes found on the banks of the St. Lawrence.

The French-language newspapers began publishing statements stating that it was only the sons of the rich or favoured families who received education at the public expense. These same newspapers kept up a constant and aggressive opposition to "The English". This process had the effect of destroying the sense of patriotism for both Quebec and Canada; it was replaced instead with a feeling of deep discontentment.

By the time Célestin Pelletier had left Kamouraska, most of the fertile lands of the old seigneuries were completely occupied and depending upon land use, the seigneurs were demanding excessively high rents. Enough sales for the use of farmlands had transpired over the years to ensure the profits to the seigneurs were well documented. John Molsen was a prominent businessman, often quoted by both the French-and English-language newspapers. Most habitants had memorized his text: "Every person who clears, or otherwise improves a farm and erects a building, bestows one-twelfth of his work and outlay on the seigneur, when the property is brought to sale. The profits which accrue to the seignior are obvious; and the vested interest of the French lawyer and notary in maintaining this system of law that fosters ongoing litigation and produces their corresponding expense is equally intelligible."

This was not news to the habitants, it was just now being stated as a public cliché. The real estate term conceded as it had been used for so many decades was now being called into question, because freehold transfer of real title was now well enough known for what it was, and as being quite different.

There is a marked difference in climate between Quebec and the eastern area near the Atlantic. Through the standard education of the time, Célestin had become acquainted with the existence of the Gulf Stream warming the eastern region. The effect of the warm water from the Gulf of Mexico pouring out into the Atlantic, flowing up the eastern coast and then making a broad circular swing back was easily calculated; as further east, the summers were balmier. The soil was also more fertile. Unbroken and inexpensive land existed; however, as in the 1800's the area known as Madawaska was not primarily farmland, but was still a forest of riotous lumber camps.

Célestin left Kamouraska, Quebec to settle in New Brunswick in1827. Being a blacksmith in this era meant that he had many choices of communities. St. Basile was his choice of location for his work and for his family home.

They had also fled a cholera epidemic. However, part of this decision to move, was more luck than planning. By the end of 1832, the cholera epidemic had claimed approximately five thousand lives in Lower Canada. In the years of 1833 to 1837, poverty and despair, due to an almost complete crop failure, was in the midst of the families of the former home region.

Célestin's move was not significant by geographical standards. They were moving over the hill to the other side of a specific major watershed. The boundary between New Brunswick and Quebec was defined by the watershed divide, between the waters that drain into the St. Lawrence River and those that drain into the Bay of Fundy. When New Brunswick was created in 1784, it had assumed these boundaries would remain from when it was a part of the previous colony of Nova

Scotia. This controversial border was due to pioneering being as much about nature as it was about politics; judgment calls about borders were the logical consequence of agriculture and the quest for freehold land.

In 1848, there was still a controversy over the control of Madawaska, the county bordering on Quebec. In 1850, two arbitrators were appointed, one by each of the provinces of Quebec and Nova Scotia. Their 1851 decision finally made adjustments to the boundary that was acceptable to both sides. The rumour quickly spread that, as only two individuals had met in private in the process, the border was created with the toss of a coin.

In fact, they had debated for many hours in front of a public viewing gallery and had arrived at no conclusions. With this impasse, they retreated to a private room. In a matter of minutes they returned with all the border issues decided. The coin flip may well have been the case, since all the detailed issues were fraught with emotional prejudice, both with and devoid of any commercial logic. A flip of a coin had possibly decided whether the Pelletier family would have lived in Quebec a further three generations.

Instead, they would now be established in New Brunswick. Whatever the methodology, the border decision was ratified by an Imperial Act of Parliament in 1851, and it would remain law.

Célestin and Justine Pelletier's sons were Rémi, Alphonse, Joseph R.P., and Thomas Henri. In all they had eleven children. Rémi is the ancestor within this tracing of lineage, character and community.

This was a time when tradition dictated that daughters were stated to be by the husband's name only upon marriage. This fact was negatively significant. Being kept invisible is one of the most serious of all actions of prejudice. The *little woman* philosophy would remain for one hundred years longer.

Alphonse Pelletier became a lawyer in Grand Falls, New Brunswick, further acquiring the title of Sir Alphonse Pelletier, PC, ICMG, CR, senator and speaker of the Senate. Later as a lawyer he resided in Quebec City. He would partake of an elite lifestyle that many in the family had not yet experienced.

Thomas Henri Pelletier was the youngest of the family. He chose to move further afield and became a doctor in Van Duren, Maine, across the international border. He lived from 1845 to 1921, and was distinguished as the first doctor to be born in St. Basile. Before moving to America, he practiced medicine in Grand Falls, New Brunswick, only a few kilometers away. Marrying the beautiful Malvina Chénard from Frenchville, Maine, would decide his destiny. In an effort to have Franco-Americans be recognized in Maine, he founded the *Journal du Madawaska* in1902. One of his sons was Reverend L.A. Pelletier, a Marist Father, who became the assistant-superior and a professor at Georgetown University, in Washington, DC.

Each brother shared one fundamental belief in common; it was that life was not as their forefathers had dictated it. Intellectual thought and discussion was a great part of these brothers' relationships with each other. That intellect shone when they met, animatedly discussing their choice of professions and reviewing the ideologies they had gleaned from their early years of communication with Célestin, their father.

Although their grandfather was determined to provide tradition by his own leadership it was always obvious that the use of individual thought was a lesson given to them. In the prior generation, Jean-Baptist had shown his offspring the need to stand up for that which they believed, while being radical in his attempts to ignore the great changes in Europe. Célestin would also use a similar approach with his family in St. Basile.

Construction began on the first community church in Saint-Basile in 1856. Made of wood, it was one of the largest in New Brunswick and was of an English Gothic style. To this small family of Pelletiers, it had an odd historical significance - it was the first local church that a Pelletier family did not help build.

In 1837, the timber-rich Madawaska region was involved in a boundary dispute between the Canadian province of New Brunswick and the American state of Maine. Lumbermen on both sides of the Saint John River fought in what became known as the Aroostook War and also as the Pork and Beans War. In 1839, both sides sent troops into the Valley of Aroostook as a part of the battle for ownership of it. The valley was the southern portion of Madawaska.

In 1839, while working with their woodcutters on the Saint-Jean River, Jean-Baptiste Daigle and his long-time friend, Joseph Nadeau, were taken prisoners by the American Commander of Fort Kent. (This is relevant to this history because, like so many families in early Canada, the Daigle family would be the next to join the Pelletier family by marriage - Jean-Baptiste Daigle's granddaughter would later marry into the Pelletier family.) The entire border conflict was resolved without serious incident through compromise culminating with the treaty of 1842. However, the five years of tug-of-war tactics between American and Canadian governments had created the concept of an independent Madawaska – a republic of Madawaska

This title of "republic" originated from a response given by a French farmer of St. Basile when a French-speaking statistician questioned him about his nationality. He was quoted as saying, "I am a citizen of the Republic of Madawaska." The name republic still stands to this day. It is joked that if a person is overly independent, he or she is possibly from Madawaska. In 1850, the Canadian Madawaska area was made up of 3,434 people and the French area of Aroostook, USA, comprised 3,000. By 1860, the population of Madawaska, New Brunswick, became 8,500.

Célestin Pelletier died on September 18, 1865 at the age of sixty-three. He passed away quietly on his clear-title farm, on Pelletier Street, St. Basile, New Brunswick. Now a urban subdivision, the farm sat in an area of gently rolling hills, on a flat plateau, next to the St. John River.

# THE RENAISSANCE MAN

Rémi Pelletier lived from 1840 to 1900. He married Philomene Martin on February 2, 1864 at St. Basile, New Brunswick; both were born and raised in this same small village in Madawaska County. They had six children: Henry, Stanley, Earnestine, Alfred, George and Joseph. Earnestine, who was the third child, died in infancy.

Upon moving to St. François as an adventurous, newly married young man, Rémi became a school teacher first, satisfying his quest for knowledge and the academic process in general. He was twenty-five years old and had been married one year. Subsequently, he became a notary public, finding this profession more gratifying to his desire for community involvement. In 1880, he opened, owned and operated the first lumber mill in the immediate area. It became the community that the Témiscouata Railroad Company would later name "Pelletier's Mill." Rémi built the sawmill beside the Crock River, which was then used for waterpower. His land also stretched a two-mile distance along the St. John River such that it could be used for log transportation.

The Pelletier's Mill school, a foresight of Rémi as a young teacher, educated nearly one hundred students a year, for almost one hundred years, until the later part of the twentieth century. The settlement would then meld into the adjacent town of St. François.

The beauty of the area is natural and the small farms of western Madawaska have developed a unique charm. The picturesque St. John River winding through the hills is framed by the casually changing seasons. The vivid colours of autumn here are not an announcement of a drab winter to follow; but the beauty lasts year-round because of the abundance of evergreen forest. Spring in particular flourishes in this serene river valley.

The forestry men of the St. John River became legendary as they drove their massive rafts of product down river to their awaiting market. *Pelletier's Mill* thrived for twenty years. It was a time of hard work, but it was also a great time of community festivities, family kinship and individual growth.

Rémi's brother, Father R.P. Joseph Pelletier, became the mission priest in the St. François area just prior to Rémi's move. When he later became the curé of St. François, Rémi donated the lumber for his new church to the community. It would be still standing one-hundred years later. Because of Rémi's community work and leadership; Pelletier's Mill, New Brunswick, the centre of most of his activity, was logically named after him. Rémi operated the mill until 1900, when he handed control of its operation to his son, George. The mill was later sold; then tragically, it was hit by lightning and burned to the ground. The disaster was a major blow for the economy of St. François; a large number of families had relied on it directly or indirectly for employment. All that is now left of the mill is an empty site in a wooded clearing. The name given to this rural community lives on.

At the turn of the nineteenth century, the area of St. François was virtually uninhabited. The first four families to arrive were those of Pascal Sirois, Rémi Pelletier, Théodore Lebel and Antoine Daigle. Their children would grow up together there, court, marry and create a large part of the community that followed. Such was life in rural Canada almost everywhere. The Pelletier families along with their neighbours would find that within their known community, almost everyone was related in some manner. This was the difference between the dynamics of the volatile west of the new dominion with a more random immigration and here in a more stable eastern community.

On July 1, 1867, The BNA Act created the Dominion of Canada and New Brunswick entered Confederation as one of the founding provinces. New Brunswick supported the union of Confederation, as did many of the other provinces because of the needed railway system. As an official community in the province, Pelletier's Mill had retained its name and became a designated rail stop.

On this July 1st, the Rémi Pelletier family, anticipating the day of the birth of their nation, gathered with their neighbours in St. François. As many walked or drove to town in buggies, clad in their Sunday best, there was a palpable air of excitement. For this major civic rendezvous the women dressed in their best gowns of bustled silks and satins.

It was the era of cute and feminine modesty; wide-brimmed bonnets, half-sheltering coy smiles and fluttering eyelashes. On the first stroke of midnight, an enormous cheer for the Queen erupted, and the large bonfire was lit. The night was not considered to be a *fait accompli* until the fire was large enough that it could be seen from other valleys. People hollered and chattered boisterously, until their enthusiasm finally sputtered into exhaustion. It was a time of great expectations. These pioneers numbered among the first 3.4 million Canadians, and a great future was presumed to be in store for them. But this lineage of the Pelletier family had been in Canada for two hundred and twenty-six years. They felt patriotic and at home.

British Columbia joined the Dominion of Canada in 1873. In 1886, the first through train of the Canadian Pacific Railway left Montreal for Port Moody, British Columbia, and the east and west future home sites of this Pelletier family were joined by transportation. Less than seventy-five years after his move from Quebec, Célestin's grandson would feel the same freedom of movement to another province, and he too would act upon it.

(Stanislaus) Stanley Claude Pelletier was born in the quiet village of St. François, New Brunswick, on a snow swept day of October 23, 1866. It was a day of family celebration- as were all the births. Pride in building a community was exceeded only by pride in family. Like generations before them, Stanley's brothers would also show themselves to each be unique individuals. In adulthood they would all try out for life in the Golden West of Canada.

Rémi's youngest son Joseph, commonly known as Joe, returned to the Pelletier's Mill community in 1902, believing that for him opportunity remained at home. Prior to his return, he had worked briefly for his two older brothers at Pelletier Lumber in the foothills of the Rocky Mountains, but his preference was the more civilized Madawaska County. He married his childhood sweetheart Edna Serios and became an elected member of the Provincial Legislative Assembly holding the position from1912 to 1916. In 1917, he left politics upon being appointed *High Sheriff*. The appointment of high sheriff was a direct appointment by the king, according to British Parliamentary law, and in this position, Joe and Edna would travel among the social elite of New Brunswick. The position involved the performance of civic duties along with jurisdiction over the justice and penitentiary system. Joseph remained high sheriff until his premature death in 1921.

Joe Pelletier has been officially credited as being one of two men who were instrumental in reclaiming French language in the Legislative Assembly. Prior to his involvement, New Brunswick had been at a crossroads over its status as being the only bilingual province in Canada.

Joe and Edna had nine children whose families moved to larger centers, following their influential father's lead.

Henry Pelletier also joined his brothers when they moved to the west. He began the operation of a brick foundry near Lethbridge, Alberta. Henry and his family sold - at a profit - and moved to Pincher Creek to become farmers. Large tracts of land were available, and this became the base of Henry's family life. Henry's wife was Philomene nee Martin and his only daughter was Ella.

George Pelletier married a *second* Edith Diagle, and later joined in partnership with Stanley by acquiring a share in the Pelletier Sawmills near Dawson Creek, British Columbia, in 1926. He also had a partnership in a sawmill in the Mill Valley or Sweetwater area, west of Dawson Creek. George and Fred Pelletier had operated a sawmill at Smithers, BC, for a time before moving to the Peace River Country in 1926. The sawmill operations were all sold in 1937, when George died at sixty-three years of age. At his funeral, it was stated that he was "generous and good-hearted to a fault and was loved the more for it".

Fred (Alfred Louis) Pelletier became an elderly bachelor who upon occasion would refuse to speak English. This eccentricity was obviously rather impractical in this small, northern, British Columbian town. Fred was born in St. Francois, New Brunswick on March 8, 1869 and he lived to be eighty years old. He died in 1949 as being fondly remembered for his stubbornness. It was said, with a northern humor, that he was so obstinate that he died "standing up straight." In actual fact he may have had a stroke or another related ailment.

Stanley Pelletier's children were Art (Arthur), Yvonne, Emile, Albertine, Jeff (Denis), and Eva. They were all born in New Brunswick. With the death of his beautiful and soft-spoken, Acadian wife, Stanley would raise the six children with only the help of his brother George and sister-in-law Edith. Art, Emile, Yvonne and Eva were sent to a boarding school at the convent in St. Basile, New Brunswick. It was located only one mile away from the small farm in which Célestin Pelletier had taken so much pride, and it was only a few miles downriver from their former home at Pelletier's Mill. Art and Emile completed their high schooling there.

Almost a century earlier, before steam engines made sailing ships obsolete, New Brunswick knew a golden age. Shipbuilding boomed in each of the villages along the beautiful tide-carved coastline. However, the golden age ended along with the opportunities that went with it. The businessmen of this period failed to make the transition to metal ships as they might have. This persistence with which the New Brunswick business community pursued and supported the wood trade and the building of wooden sailing ships, even in the face of technological obsolescence, became obvious by the 1890s. It was an ill-conceived commitment to a declining economic base, but it may have been understandable in such small resource-based village economies as St. François and Pelletier's Mill. However, it was more difficult to comprehend in the context of the complex, differentiated economy that existed in St. John. Unfortunately, the merchants of this city of 27,000 possessed a monopoly over the commerce of the Saint John River Valley and its tributaries, which was now made up of a market of 100,000 people. This included Madawaska County.

A total of four generations of the Stanley Pelletier family lived in New Brunswick, with Célestin settling in1827, and Rémi Pelletier, living there throughout his life. Stanley's children were all born there. Almost as a second-generation tradition now, at the death of his father in 1900, Stanley set out to find opportunity in the Alberta and British Columbia Rocky Mountain foothills. As was also traditional in finding opportunity, Alberta was not yet an official province.

The west would challenge them all. Edith Pelletier joined Stanley in that challenge; however, she would shortly return to her beloved New Brunswick to pass away.

# CHAPTER 9 - ACADIAN ROOTS

Stanley Pelletier had married an Acadian. History would define Acadia in an ongoing fashion. She was almost the girl next door. Actually she lived in the next village, and her name was Edith Diagle. Edith was born at St. Hilaire, New Brunswick on March 12, 1875. After a life kept interesting by the adventurous Stanley, she died January 18, 1909, while giving birth to her daughter Eva. She had lived on both sides of the new dominion of Canada with their young family. Befitting of that challenge, and among the excitement of their lives, they had shared the adventure of being very close to the infamous Frank Slide in Western Canada, as it roared into the quiet night. She had been a dynamic lady.

The decision of whether to save the mother or the child was an all too common one during this period. The priest would make the decision of death, as the church ruled that the child should always be saved first. As the head of his family, Stanley would become somewhat distant from his church later in his life. He would send his children to Catholic school; however he would only do this on the condition that they would be schooled in both languages. The Pelletier family always would retain a great respect for their mother and her ultimate sacrifice. The fact that it was a way of life for many of the women of early Canada, to die in childbirth was never spoken of overtly. Death, like history, was simply accepted as a natural rhythm of nature, in a time when nature was still considered more powerful than medicine.

Sacrifice was not unique to being Acadian; it was a part of life in general. Edith's Acadian ancestors had settled in their brave new world two hundred years earlier. An uncle by the name of Oliver Daigle (with the last name changed from D'Aigre) farmed and had registered land in 1707. He was a twenty-eight-year old ploughman during a 1671 census near the settlement of Rivière-au-Dauphin, about four miles from Port Royal. At that time there were 1,400 Acadians in Canada, most of them found within communities on the larger marshes near what was then called the Baie Française. It later became the Bay of Fundy.

Simon Daigle had settled in Canada, in the area that is now Nova Scotia, in the eighteenth century for specific reasons common to his life and time. He came from Normandy or Bretonne, in France. France at the time was by far the richest country in Europe, but it also had the largest population of any of the Western European nations. In France, further expansion of farmland was not possible, as the aristocracy owned approximately thirty percent of all of the land. As taxes increased beyond the possibility of payment, many families lost their land, as did Simon Daigle and his family.

Upon arriving in the New World, these first Acadians were anxious to succeed in what they perceived as a great opportunity. They ingeniously had saved themselves the time and labour of clearing the wooded uplands; instead, they used the lowlands and marshlands around the numerous small rivers that drained into the bays. They then built dykes to protect their fields from high tides. In doing so they learned to produce exceptional crops and fine marsh hay.

These dykes were more than three meters wide and at least two meters high. They were made of stones and logs and were packed with clay. Built into the base of the dyke were sluices called *aboiteaux*. These were wooden boxes with clapper valves hinged to seaward. This prevented seawater from entering at high tide while allowing the marshes to drain at low tide. Frequently they built roads along the tops of these dykes. However, within the period of Simon's great-grandson, Augustin Justin Daigle would entirely change to the method of highland farming. The new method required clearing the fields in a tried and tested manner of hard labour. It was always said that the fertile soil of the marshes held a much greater yield than was gained after the family's move to the highlands.

Their principal crops were wheat and legumes supplemented by oats, rye, barley and flax. Cattle were the dominant livestock; however, they would also keep pigs, poultry and sheep for wool.

In 1713, the name of Acadia was changed to Nova Scotia. It did not seem like an important event to the individuals on the farms of Acadia. More important to them was that there was no major shortage of food between 1713 and 1748. They no longer experienced the former plight of the years of the early 1600s where half of the settlers died from cold and scurvy. Shelter was readily available, clothing was adequate and above all, there were no major epidemics. Even when the plague did reach the colony, its ravages were confined, both in 1709 and 1751, almost exclusively to the garrisons of the troops.

Parish records of Grand Pré show that of 174 marriages for which detailed information is available, one-third involved partners either from elsewhere in the colony or from abroad. Sixteen of them were from France, another eight from Quebec and three from Cape Breton. It seems probable that Simon, in fact, was a Frenchman in need of a wife and love. His life in Acadia would provide both.

There was a time in history when Acadia was to be developed into its own nation. The flag of Acadia, which is a French tricolour with a yellow star in a blue field, now flies proudly at Grand Pré National Historic Park. The park is the main site of their largest expulsion in 1755, and is restored as authentically as possible to the times and the styles of Simon and Madeleine. Simon was not living inside the village as his future wife Madeleine Gautrea was, but they met while he had visited for basic supplies.

Jean Daigle, their son, was born at his family's temporary working accommodations on Île St. Croix. They subsequently moved back to the area of the Nova Scotia mainland and to Port Royal, living there until 1773. Fortune favoured them in being able to leave the area together, amid the confusion of the ongoing Acadian deportation by the British. They left with their young son Joseph. The next two decades would find the small family without a farm, a home or even consistent shelter.

Theirs was the time of thatched-roofed houses, built of oak and hemlock, with second-story dormer windows and large gables projecting out emphatically. Traces of the French Baroque style existed in both the layout of the village and with the use of the local materials - wood and clay. Madeleine Daigle can be imagined spinning flax for the loom, churning butter and making cheese while wearing her traditional Norman cap. The men wore wooden shoes, which were also traditional from their former homeland in France. Some of the villagers had imported their tradition of farming from the Burgundian vineyards in France.

The seasons imposed harsh demands for immediate labour, for seeds to be sown, crops gathered, fish caught and wood cut, all entirely dependent upon weather conditions. Cabbage, turnips, peas, beans, onions and corn were the popular vegetables, as they were all hardy and easily stored. The year also brought festivities and holidays. The Acadians kept the twelve days of Christmas, the customs of Candlemas and the celebrations common to Easter. Long winter evenings allowed card playing, dancing, pipe smoking, storytelling and singalongs. The spring and summer months would see the celebrations of weddings and many new births. Thus evolved a life distinctive enough to provide the sustenance for a continuing Acadian identity to be remembered.

The Acadians were separated from Canada by a vast distance with impenetrable forests, and as a result they were left to their own resources without immigration and assistance. The two founding countries, France and England, had aided other parts of Canada; however, no assistance existed for Acadia. Whatever assistance England or France ought to have provided might well have been proportionate to the impending dangers of this harsh war theatre between them.

Had the Acadians been less isolated, they might have been more politically aware of events in other parts of Canada. They also might have been more sensitive to the precarious situation the British faced concerning the continuing threat from France. There was also almost no communication between territories otherwise they may have offered a necessary pledge of allegiance to the British. The Acadians assumed the British would accept their continued non-allegiance and allow them to simply carry on their business of planting and reaping. However, in 1764, representatives of 165 Acadian families, which included 1,000 people, finally did take the oath.

At this time, that the Daigles were split apart from their neighbours who would inadvertently choose to be entangled in the last years of deportation. The Daigles had declared themselves loyal and were thus now given the right to live elsewhere in the colony. This allowed them a free movement away from Port Royal, as long as they agreed to give up their land. Many battles would be fought in this new land, but these were not the battles of the Acadians themselves. The expulsion of Acadians from the Nova Scotia area came in the aftermath of these disputes and was a case of local British over-reacting to security concerns arising from the perceived military threat from France.

The troubles began immediately in 1604 with the establishment of Acadia, the first permanent settlement in the New World. They would not end. The tiny French community began with eighty people. A ten-year fur trade monopoly for the region was granted to one of the Protestant founders, on the understanding that he would establish a French colony of Catholics in the area of the Bay of Fundy. Because of this strategic location of Acadia near the Gulf of St. Lawrence, England and France continually fought for its possession. The region changed hands frequently until 1713.

Acadia existed with ill-defined boundaries between all the expanding empires of New France and New England. Their southern community in present-day Maine had been destroyed in 1613 by its local war. The Acadians responded logically to this precarious situation by adopting an attitude of being border people with a determined focus on tending their farms. They well understood that it was useless for them to attempt to deal with political situations over which they had no control. In the 1670s they numbered fewer than five hundred people on what is now peninsular Nova Scotia. Tiny settlements also began to be established on Prince Edward Island and New Brunswick.

The Acadians had now known a relatively lengthy and legitimate period of English rule from 1654 to 1668. There were also a number of more brief periods of English control as a result of raids out of Massachusetts. The American colonies were anxious about the growing power of France in Canada, and it was their stated position to carry out what they called "The Glorious Enterprise" proposed by their leaders, which had for its aim the extermination of French authority on the continent.

Although the Acadians themselves were not known for acts of piracy or warfare, they had supplied neighbouring bands of Indians with firearms that were used in raids on New England colonies. The colonies not only blamed Acadia for these raids, but also for a series of raids originating from New France.

A force consisting of English and New England volunteers attacked Port Royal consistently. In 1710 they finally achieved victory. They had conquered a community that was in great poverty at a time when France was close to bankruptcy as a nation.

By 1700, the Acadians were as accustomed to dealing with the officials of England as much as those of France. The subsequent continual transfers of the colony were perceived by the uninvolved farmers to be just another step in a complicated ritual. It was the exchange of France's control over them to England's, which was something that had occurred before and that would likely be reversed in the not too distant future, by their estimation.

The Treaty of Utrecht had confirmed British control of Nova Scotia in 1713, and the Daigle family became fully aware of their personal choice of living under British rule. The treaty contained a provision allowing the Acadians up to a year to leave with their possessions, should they wish to leave the colony. In 1713, Acadia was home to eighteen hundred peaceful farmers, most of whom had decided to remain on their land. By 1730, the Acadian population had doubled. This group included Simon Daigle.

However, it was the frequent changing of hands regarding control of Acadia that led the Acadians to the false assumption that they should strive not to offend either warring power. This fundamental belief in the probability of continuing alternate French and English control of the colony became the cornerstone of Acadian logic. From the Acadian perspective, it would have been folly to engage in any action that might bind them irrevocably to one great power - when the other still had vested interests in the future status of the colony and its inhabitants.

In all, ten decades of war would be the final realization. The oath of King George I was rejected outright, with later oaths taken to King George II, but in circumstances that allowed Acadians to believe they had been granted the right to remain neutral. Given Acadia's status as a tiny, under-populated colony compared with its neighbours, they understandably wanted to avoid direct conflict with these far more powerful forces.

On being asked to pledge for an oath of allegiance to King George I, the Annapolis Royal Acadians refused, citing matters of religious freedom that were not yet clarified. Secondly was the danger from the Indians, who would likely disapprove of friendship between the Acadians and the English. The refusal was an unwillingness to take an oath that they would neither take up arms against his Britannic Majesty nor against France, nor against their subjects or allies. It followed that both the English and the French, when referring to Acadians from 1730 onward, often called them "the Neutral French." This suggests the Acadian's neutrality was generally tolerated and may even have been warmly accepted by both sides.

Post-treaty Acadia was a land fraught with problems for Britain to the extent that it began to consider the possibility of entirely removing the Catholic and French Acadians. The Daigle family became directly involved in this process, as the English would end the difficulties inherent in governing a land where they spoke a different language and practiced a different religion.

Acadians also outnumbered the local British garrisons charged with keeping the peace in Acadia. Part of the British dilemma was that a massive departure of Acadians and their livestock would crush the colony's economy, destroy the local fur trade and disrupt sources of food and labour needed to sustain the British garrison. It was also felt that any large departure of Acadians would likely migrate to Cape Breton Island, where they would bolster the already strong French threat posed by the fortress town of Louisbourg. The fortress had been constructed in 1713 and for a short time it represented a promise of opportunity for French-speaking settlers.

When a number of Acadian families decided to leave Acadia during the first year of the treaty, Governor Philips intended to stop them. They were not permitted to depart on British vessels if by chance they were able to board. He next permitted them to swear an oath of non- aggression, as quite different from an oath of allegiance to Britain.

In 1744, when hostilities broke out between the English and the French in Mascarene, the lieutenant-governor of the colony wrote to London that had the Acadians not remained neutral, the colony would have fallen to the French. He further wrote that this policy had procured nearly thirty-five years of peace for their communities..

With a revival of hostility between France and England, Nova Scotia's lieutenant-governor, Charles Lawrence, and his council at Halifax insisted that the Acadians finally take the unconditional oath of allegiance to the British Crown. By 1755, Acadia had been British for forty-two years and almost its entire population- including the Daigle family- had been born

British subjects. However, when they refused to take the oath, the nervous British Officials decided to act with the deportation order. Their perceptions of Acadian loyalty were various. This was the beginning of the Seven Year's War between England and France. Two thousand immigrants from England and fifteen hundred more from Germany arrived in Halifax, the newly founded capital of Nova Scotia. This gave the British an immediate population of hand-picked citizens equal to nearly half the population of the Acadians, who now numbered eight thousand. Two facts were now relevant. Firstly, simply allowing additional waves of non-Acadian immigration to take place could have erased any remaining threat from the Acadians. However, secondly, the deportation of the Acadians was now carried out without any approval from London England.

The deportation order affected 13,000 Acadians within this extended community. This vast majority of Acadians had never taken up arms against the British, even when it would have been to their possible advantage to do so. They had a lengthy, proven history of nonviolent coexistence with the British. This was exemplified by their refusal to accept French invitations and threats to attack the British, their role as suppliers of food and labour to a vulnerable garrison and their acceptance of British rule – all combined with aiding Britain's eventual position of extreme dominance in the region of New England, and northward. Any minority of Acadians who were guilty of crimes against the British might have been dealt with judiciously without Lawrence ever having to expel the entire peaceful population.

Considering the Acadians were French- speaking Catholics with relatives in both New France and France, the neutrality they had offered the British was likely the best possible arrangement the British could have hoped for - as it should also have been obvious that the Acadians could not reasonably have been expected to take up arms against their own French kin.

When requested, the Acadians willingly turned over their weapons to the British, who were surprised to find more than two thousand hunting rifles within the group. The Acadians could easily have conquered the small British garrison of about two hundred men. They also relinquished their boats and any strongholds on the coast. It would often be stated that these two facts of non-violence proved the expulsion was an unnecessary tragedy. Further, the expulsion order was particularly controversial because it took place after the British had captured Fort Beausejour at the foot of the Bay of Fundy. With this, the French threat in Nova Scotia had been entirely removed.

A single individual, Governor Charles Lawrence, had made the deportation decision. As a result, he earned the contempt, not only of the Acadians, but also of many others in Halifax who devoted passages of their correspondence to describing his arrogant nature. They included mention of his vile disposition and his inability to tolerate anyone who held an opinion different from his own. It might be said that he was the ultimate lone fascist.

Lieutenant-Colonel John Winslow, as the officer in charge of the logistics of the deportation, recorded the actual scene and his specific speech made on the day of the expulsion. He has often been quoted and the scene has been replayed repeatedly over time. Four hundred and eighteen Acadian men had been crowded into the parish church as he acted on his plan of enforcement. The Daigle family was not involved as they were departing peacefully. As is often the case in historic recounting of a tale, the more emotional scenes are the focus. However, many Acadian families had decided simply to move as was requested. They were first and second generations in New France, and their families had survived and had worked in a feudal system of usury and abuse for centuries. Leaving and starting over was not as difficult as much of the rhetoric of the expulsion period would embellish. Agricultural, social and even political systems in New France were still a significant improvement over the quality of life in the old country.

Simon Daigle and his young family were among those who escaped the deportation. Because they had immigrated toward the settlements along the St. Lawrence River, they were among the 165 families who would be counted as having remained in the area of Acadia, their total population becoming fewer than one thousand people.

The old willow trees in Grand Pré National Historic Park are said to have survived from the time the Daigles met there as a couple. An ivy- covered chapel in the park now commemorates the former church in which the expulsion notice was read. A century later, the American poet Henry Wadsworth Longfellow was to immortalize the era with "Evangeline: A Tale of Acadie." With its memorial opening of, "This is the forest primeval," this epic poem told the dramatic story of the dispersal of the Acadians. Millions of individuals have since come to know the story of Evangeline's romance with Gabriel, their forced separation and her lifelong search for her lover. Longfellow wrote that on their marriage day all of the Acadian men of the province were summoned to their parishes to hear the proclamation being read.

As the poem states, "Naught but tradition remains of the beautiful village of Grand Pré. This was a reference to the fact that the British soldiers under orders from Winslow, had immediately burned down the village. Knowing that other villages in other places and at other times had also been decimated deliberately by fire, many families such as the Daigles would carry on successfully despite having to begin anew yet one more time.

Originally 1,300 Acadians escaped to Quebec, while others went temporarily to Ile Royale. Yet others were captured, beaten and sent to France or England. By 1759, approximately 1,500 Acadians had gone into the forests creating many clusters of Acadian enclaves. By 1765, all the former lands farmed by the Daigle family and their contemporaries, were occupied by newcomers. For the most part the farms of the Acadians would later to be dispensed to United Empire Loyalists. As free grants, these homesteads were a reward for staying loyal to Britain against the American Revolution. The simultaneous Loyalist influx of forty thousand people needed and used enormous quantities of their former land.

For many Acadians, deportation was only the beginning of their wanderings. Many of those sent to the British colonies along the Atlantic seaboard traveled further onto Louisiana or to the West Indies. A few went to South America. In 1785, more than 1,500 Acadian refugees, having gone to France, now immigrated to Louisiana. One-third or more of the exiles that had reached Boston, Philadelphia, South Carolina or the British seaports, died from smallpox, yellow fever or typhoid. Within all these groups some invariably found their way back to Acadia, either to be deported again or to settle in areas little suited to farming. For this reason the Daigle family like many, were to farm for two generations on land largely unsuitable for any type of agriculture.

In 1783, an official government group was sent to examine the region of the Saint John River and to make a report on the colonization of the New Brunswick area. The report indicated the exact state of the small colony of d'Ecoupag, which was the most flourishing of the Acadian establishments, and it was here that the Daigles had settled. The years since the expulsion were fraught with difficulties; survival was often on a day-to-day basis only. Sixty-one families were counted for a total of 357 people. This same document lists all of the heads of families who had given their services to the British government during the American-English War. Six men are listed as having actually taken part, with Joseph Daigle being one of them. Joseph was Simon Daigle's son, born in the region of Grand Pré and then serving in adulthood as a combatant for the British.

In this document these colonists were recommended being given a favor, each commended as having "served with unshaken loyalty", signed by the governor. The commendation created a new scenario and a different type of eviction for this group of Acadians. The "favour" bestowed upon them for their loyalty was to be relocated to the region of Madawaska and abandoning their little settlement, which is now Fredericton.

They would use canoes, rafts and any other means available to move to Madawaska on the Saint John River.

In the series S, Volume 1784 of the Canadian Archives, the requests shown are specific. A list of twenty-four of the names of the heads of families who had asked for ownership of land in Madawaska includes both Joseph Simon Daigle and his son Jean Baptiste Daigle, who could now enjoy this beautiful valley.

During this last exodus, Acadia had all but disappeared, and the area that is now the three Maritime Provinces, became the British colony of Nova Scotia. In 1784, the separate province of New Brunswick was formed. The Daigle family and their community were now farming the land; however, they had not yet obtained official title. On June 21, 1785, Joseph Daigle again wrote to the Governor General of Canada, this time asking for other titles to the land in Madawaska. He also asked for two cents per acre for the farms taken from them previously.

Governor Carlton had come to know Joseph well; and he often referred to him as the "gentleman farmer," in a positive context. He also referred to Joseph as one of the most interesting figures of this pioneer group. This may have been due to Joseph's ability to write in the embellished style of the period as well as his well-known integrity and hospitality.

More than one book has made reference to the correspondence between the governor and Joseph Daigle; however, in a book called Canada and Its Provinces (published in 1913 by the Edinburgh University Press;) specific reference is made to an often-used quote from the letters of Joseph Daigle. Even though he had experienced many vicissitudes when called upon by Governor Carlton, one of these being to abandon the fields his hands had worked, he had exclaimed: "Can it be that the good God has no place on earth for the Acadians?" This quote has been referred to as everything from "pathetic" - that is, being too passive, to "very inspirational" – that is, being a devout believer and a good citizen. Neither assumption can be entirely correct.

Joseph Daigle arrived in Madawaska in June of 1785 and purposely, after the fashion of Jacque Cartiers so many years before him, stepped ashore and planted a cross in the soil of their new land. Dressed in full panoply similar to that of Cartier, whose cross also had been erected with great ceremony, men had dropped to their knees and raised their arms toward the heavens in a gesture of humility and praise. Unfortunately within a few months the tall beam with its ornate carving soon began to collapse from the force of strong winds, until it finally fell into the soil. However, the story of that impressive moment when the cross was elevated against the Canadian backdrop of green trees and blue skies, would be re-enacted when a durable commemorative cross was erected by the Historical Society two hundred years later, in 1985. Direct reference was made to Joseph Daigle as the former community leader and cross bearer. The site is also shown in the National Registry of Historic Sites in Maine, U.S.A. Attempts such as this, at reinstating pride, were very successful.

The cross as a symbol was all that was left to this ancestor and his people. France had abandoned them and their English conquerors had left them with no hope of future. The forest had proved to be inhospitable, most Indian nations were less than enthusiastic about their arrival, and the elements seemed consistently to provide only misery.

During that summer of 1785, Acadians chose their farms and began to improve the land. Their first concern was to plant potatoes and wheat. They had arrived with very little in the way of tools and had been given no compensation for their former farms or produce.

A petition was made by Joseph Daigle and Paul Potier claiming against these injustices:

*Fredericton, February 22, 1786*
*To His Excellency Governor Carlton:*
*Your Memorialists are reduced to a most deplorable condition with their numerous families for want of provisions, some having been under the necessity of selling the few cattle they had, to prevent them from starving.*

*They are the Memorial of the French Inhabitants who have been deprived of their lands by disbanded English soldiers as also has Joseph Daigle and Paul Potier now residing in Madawaska.*

*That the Memorialists thus circumstanced are under the necessity of having recourse to Your Excellency for redress of their miseries."*

The outcome of this petition was a right to the title of their farmlands. These titles were obtained partly by the right of possession and partly by purchase. Joseph Daigle's lobbying had proved to be successful. The economic setback was temporary; within two years this new colony was established with log homes built, huge fireplaces providing warmth and functional furniture conducive to evenings of family togetherness. Utensils and plates were made of wood and meat was entirely provided by hunting and fishing. The fall of 1786 had also bestowed the first in a series of plentiful wheat harvests.

Also in 1786, church construction was completed. Joseph became the church warden over this and later another church. Historians would later refer to him as both the "Father of the Colony," and "the pillar and foundation of the birth of the church in Madawaska." The first marriage at the Madawaska Church was cause for great excitement among the Daigle family. Simon Hebert married Joseph's daughter, Josephte Daigle.

In June 1790, a new and larger church was completed. Thirty-five by fifty-five feet, of unusual proportions, it was made up of large rooms squared, with pew rows of varying angles, and it boasted a large cross and high bell tower. This was a time of great celebration. After the first mass, Joseph Daigle, now an elderly man, having inspired, arranged and coordinated the church construction, handed over his office to his successor, Alexandre Albert. Joseph declared with legitimate pride that the construction was now entirely paid for. He symbolically put the sixty-nine gold pieces left over into a case. He then gave this to their priest for his numerous personal services. With this ceremony the existence of Madawaska and freedom for these Acadians, now seemed assured!

Two hundred years later, one of his offspring, the author and his great-great-great grandson Lonnie Pelletier, was to use the same methodology as his ancestor by building a church of almost exactly the same dimensions. Both men were project managers during construction, while simultaneously dealing with the challenge of interfacing with the unusual aspirations of their local congregations. In each case, a willingness to sacrifice personal ego for the betterment of the group was required. Each church was located very near the shores of the two opposite oceans, the Atlantic and the Pacific.

\*\*\*

Acadian food specialties handed down from the life and times of Joseph Daigle are still offered in various restaurants today. Pot-en-pot is a chicken stew cooked with homemade noodles, and Poutines Rapees are made up of large balls of grated and mashed potatoes embedded with diced salt pork and simmered in water. They are served with salt and pepper for a main course, or with molasses for a tasty dessert. Other dishes combined turnips, cabbages or red beans with bacon.

\*\*\*

Jean Baptiste Daigle, Joseph's son, married Marie Trahan and they produced four children. He continued to farm the land, initially broken by his father, from 1779 on. With great determination and tenacity, he attempted to create a substantial farm from the inferior soil conditions. But perseverance did not pay off; the 1831 census listed this parcel as "dejected but not yet burnt out," this being at a time before fertilizers were available for the soil. Better trained in clearing and farming techniques than his father, he finally relocated a few miles away in 1819 expanding the family farm by four times its original size.

The third church in Madawaska began construction in 1811 and was completed in1818. Jean-Baptiste Daigle was the church warden and one of a group of three men that provided the construction management for the project.

In 1831, Madawaska was incorporated and a detailed census was taken, including a summary of all buildings and cultivated lands. The census listed much of the land as cleared and cultivated and included many timber houses. Numerous family members had now settled on Daigle Island. Sylvain Daigle was taking care of his father, Joseph Daigle, now an elderly man, and Jean-Baptiste Daigle was one of the citizens winning a seat in the first local municipal council elections.

Augustin could never have envisioned that the home that he built in 1848 would become a provincial museum due to both its durability and accompaniments, some one hundred and fifty years later. Augustin's son Zepherin Daigle continued farming, and a monument to his memory was later erected on his land.

In the course of its first century, the Madawaska settlement, which had begun with just twenty-four families, had grown into a community of twenty-four thousand people! Two cousins with the same name, from the Daigle family, would marry into the Pelletier family. Edith Daigle married George Pelletier and her cousin Edith Daigle married Stanley Pelletier.

With these two remarkable women, the Pelletier family could carry on. They sacrificed their lives for family and like many before, they were willing to give their life for births.

# Chapter 10 - Front Line Battle

The First World War was unnecessary. The chain of events that led to its outbreak might have been broken at any point during the five weeks of diplomatic crises that preceded the first shot. Its tragedy is that ten million human beings subsequently died and the emotional lives of millions more were destroyed within these four years. It left a legacy of political turmoil and racial hatred so intense that no explanation of the causes of the Second World War can stand without reference to the first.

However, the fact is that for the majority of working people in Canada, the war was but a passage in their lives, an interruption of normality to which society rapidly returned as soon as silence had fallen on its many fronts.

But in Europe and elsewhere outside of North America, the medieval value system of social hierarchy of human beings still predominated. Generals began to use thousands of soldiers per day as pawns. In the civilian world, conditions of labour were evolving into a new philanthropic concern. In an age of mass immigration, local governments found themselves unable to regulate the welfare of those seeking a new life in other chosen and distant lands.

The restriction of working hours and the unethical employment of children began to become a major influence on much domestic legislation in many European states, but during the nineteenth century only a handful of countries had begun to give it substantial recognition. By the start of World War I in 1914, many European states had entered into bilateral treaties protecting workers. For example, there were now human rights for social insurance and industrial compensation, and simultaneously the restriction of female and child labour. This could be seen as a government response to the activities of international workingmen's movements, particularly the First International, of only two decades earlier.

It had been founded by Karl Marx in London and Paris. These newly initiated laws; however, did nothing to protect the soldiers from being used in the most callous of ways as they served in the war.

Among the other great industrial enterprises of Europe at the turn of the twentieth century, the industry of creating soldiers flourished. All leading European countries had accepted the necessity of submitting their young men to military training in early manhood and of requiring them to remain at the government's disposition as reservists into their late years of maturity. This resulted in producing enormous armies of both serving and potential soldiers. The unintended consequences created a second, submerged and invisible military society, inside European civil society. Millions of strong men shouldered a rifle, marched in step, and learned to obey orders without a second thought.

European generals, unconcerned with the spirits of their troops or the reasoning of their governments, were passionate about theoretical placements of armies on a map. For most of these leaders, war had been reduced to pure abstraction with the allocation of corps a paramount concern. As a prime example, in retrospect, it could be seen that the primary objective of these calculations was not an effort to equalize French to German troops, but simply to identify the volume of soldier traffic the Belgian and French road network could physically accommodate. Such calculations were the groundwork of an officer's academic training, which was that of transferring from prepared tables the length of a marching column, to a road map. This could determine how many troops could be pushed through a given sector and at what speed. The variable of any human resistance was simply a calculation.

By 1914, a net of interlocking and opposing understandings with mutual assistance treaties were in place. France would go to war on Russia's side and vice versa if either were attacked by Germany. Austria, Hungary and Italy were dubbed the Triple Alliance and over lunch they decided that Austria could rely on Germany's full support against Serbia and with Bulgaria. During the dessert of the meal, Russian intervention was discussed but discounted. Such were the discussions in the higher echelons of the offices of government ministers, ambassadors and military advisors.

In reality, the ignorance and misunderstanding among politicians and diplomats of how the abstract war plans, once instigated, would operate was the biggest barrier to any peace accord that might have been achieved. Those few logically thinking leaders who fully comprehended the trigger effect exerted by one mobilization proclamation on another, and the inflexibility of deployment once begun, were ignored as being too philosophical.

At the start of the Great War not only were political philosophies from the past century outdated, so too were the uniforms. This seemed an unintended symbolism. The French and Austrian armies both prepared for war in 1914 garbed much as they had been in 1870. The heavy cavalry of the French wore brass helmets with a long horsehair plume and the light cavalry wore frogged jackets and scarlet trousers. Some of the heavy cavalry were further burdened with breastplates also unchanged in both weight and pattern from the time of Waterloo under Napoleon.

The light cavalry of the African Army were dressed in heavy sky-blue tunics and the Spanish in flowing red cloaks. Others were clad in baggy red breeches and Turkish waistcoats or even turned-back blue greatcoats with legs encased in bright-red trousers tucked into calf-length boots. All these uniforms were made of heavy wool. Their enormous weight proved to be one of many additional ordeals of combat throughout the hot summers.

The Russians, however, were unexpectedly modern with their olive-green overshirt and simulated athletic tunics. Both the Germans and the British had made a new start with new uniforms, both of which were field-gray. In the German army reference was made to tradition by way of double-breasted tunics, with frogging or spiked helmets depending on the branch of service. In almost all armies little patches of colour, or in the case of the British, a tartan, distinguished regiment from regiment.

The uniform included the weight of a rifle of ten pounds, a bayonet, a trenching tool, ammunition pouches holding a hundred rounds or more, a water bottle, a larger pack containing spare socks and shirt, and a haversack with iron containers for rations and field dressing. No infantryman's marching load weighed less than sixty pounds above that of his initial uniform, and it had to be carried for an expected thirty kilometres per day. In this war, feet were as important as trains or horses.

Even in the initial stages of war, the infantry men who were given no opportunity to ride would often drop behind the column or route. In grim determination they hobbled along in ones and twos seeking desperately to stay in touch with their regiments. Food came up from Army Service Corps ration dumps, which were often just boxes of biscuits or tins of bully beef. In actual fact they even achieved marching forty kilometers on many good days.

A friend of Emile Pelletier had been separated from his platoon and later summed up the thoughts of these men of the front lines:

*"I came across some more of our fellows and one officer. Once we'd got together and were deciding what to do, a German officer came crawling through the bushes. When he saw us he said, 'I am wounded'– in perfect English. Our officer said to him, 'You shouldn't make those bloody attacks, then you wouldn't get wounded'. It gave us a laugh! Anyway we bandaged him up, waited there and shortly afterwards our officer was killed by a stray bullet, so we had no officers then. All you could hear was some firing going on, but I didn't know where the devil I was really. The German died then. I covered him over with leaves and twigs, anything I could scoop up just there. Then I crawled back to rejoin our unit."*

On the Eastern Front both sides became worn down by the harshness of the elements and the fruitlessness of their efforts. The men were often cut to pieces and became defenseless. The wounded who could not drag themselves off the battlefield, were left to die.

On the Western Front trench warfare became a specific methodology. This earthwork barrier stretched for 1,300 miles. Barbed wire had been invented in the 1870s and appeared, strung in belts between the opposing trenches. In wet or stony ground the trenches were shallow, with a higher parapet to the front. Because they were built of earth they were usually sandbagged. The drier and more workable the soil, the less need there was for supporting the internal trench walls. Some of them developed into stair-cased shelters that were thirty feet deep or more.

A no man's land was usually two or three hundred metres wide. Intense trench fighting could produce an international barbed wire barrier to be mended by both sides. New trenches were always being dug to improve the line or repair stretches lost infighting. The Western Front would shortly become a maze of duplicates and dead ends in which soldiers easily lost their way. Guides who knew the trench geography were an essential accompaniment. As rain fell, the trenches filled with water. The winter would create floods, and the ditch would then turn into liquid mud and become a stream. This in turn opened into a river, which had to be abandoned unless it could be built up above the water level with timbers. Building and rebuilding was all accomplished while under enemy fire.

A few kilometres away, an abrupt transition occurred from the trenches of death to normal life, all the more so pronounced because prosperity reigned in the rear areas (from the front-lines). The armies had brought money and the shops and cafés flourished. In the zone of German occupation was an austere economic regime driving the coalmines, cloth mills and ironworks at full speed for the Reich. Outside this ribbon of destruction the roads were full of traffic with long lines of horse and motor transport. Civilian fields were ploughed by the farmers rights up to the line were the shells fell. New towns of tents and huts sprang up to accommodate the millions who went up and down to the trenches, almost as if on a factory shift. It was usually four days in the front line, four in support, four at rest. Emile Pelletier's diary mirrored this schedule.

While training their peacetime militia, the Territorial Force, for active service, the British had created an entire new army of volunteers. Together these would produce nearly sixty divisions, in addition to those from Canada and Australia that were hastening across the Atlantic and Pacific to the motherland's aid.

As a volunteer, Emile Pelletier had joined the 21st Reserve Battalion, shortly after they were a part of the assault at Vimy Ridge. This battle was on September 25, 1915, when six British divisions were stopped by machine guns, the 21st and the 14th Battalions started forward in support. In the early afternoon they moved forward in ten columns, each of about a thousand men, all advancing as if carrying out a parade-ground drill. The sight of an entire front covered with the enemy's infantry astounded the German defenders. They stood up, some even venturing onto the parapet of their trenches and fired triumphantly into the mass of Canadians advancing across the open grassland. The barrels of their machine guns became hot and swimming in oil, as they traversed back and forth along the Canadians' ranks. Opening fire at about 1,500 meters range, one machine gun alone fired 12,500 rounds that afternoon.

The Canadians fell by the hundreds, but they continued their march relentlessly and with great discipline, until they reached the unbroken wire of the Germans' second position. Here the Canadian survivors finally turned to retire back. The German enemies, nauseated by the spectacle of this field of Canadian corpses, held their fire as they turned to retreat. German records would state it differently as: "so great was the feeling of compassion and mercy after such a victory."

Of the 15,000 infantry of the 21st and 24th Divisions, over 8,000 had been killed or wounded. One of the majors wrote to his wife in the usual understated way: "the main thing is to kill plenty of Huns with as little loss to oneself as possible; it's a great game and our allies are playing it top hole." It would still be several years before the deluge of pointless losses quenched the enthusiasm of either army.

Emile Pelletier joined the 21st Reserve Battalion on August 3rd to March to do battle at Boulogne (August 5), Etaples (August 7), and Agnes les Duisans (August 9) followed by Wancourt, Marquion and Haynecourt.

Having rejoined the 31st Battalion he stated in his diary that they were "in close supports for two days." On September 12th they marched to Monchecourt, where they remained for three weeks. They then joined the lines at Denain and Valenciennes.

On this dreary day in hell, the Canadian corps finally captured the town of Valenciennes. Emile's diary carried on from his initial description of the marches and battles in France. After Vimy, Lieutenant General Sir Arthur Currie provided the Canadian leadership. Emile joined his battalion and was with them when they freed Cambria and caused the fall of Valenciennes on November 1st.

"From Valenciennes crossed Belgium border to Quievrechain, on the 8th of November through Dour Frameries," wrote Emile.

When crossing ground that was subsequently captured, bodies of soldiers wounded a month earlier were found. These soldiers had crawled into shell holes, wrapped their waterproof sheets around them, taken out their bibles and had then died. They were among thousands whose bullet-riddled bodies gave up life beyond the reach of stretcher-bearers or who were simply lost in the wilderness of no man's land. Even among those found and carried back, many died as they lay waiting for treatment outside the field hospitals, which were too overwhelmed to provide service.

In these early November days, the weather was wet and chilly, very different from the bright August when these troops had last fought in this region. The original forces of the group that had taken the shock of Germany's first fury were either dead or prisoners or crippled for life, and the rest had been dispersed throughout the whole British army. Emile now found himself among the famous first five divisions that created the retreat from Mons. It now consisted of mainly new men.

Emile continued in his diary:

*"From Frameries, Belgium, we left at three o'clock in the morning, walking eight kilometers to the front line, relieving the 20$^{th}$ Battalion. We reached the line at five o'clock. Fought till the last minute at eleven o'clock our time. We took Havre'Ville, on the right of Mons, and a wood on the right of the village. Then all stopped, by the armistice. All was quiet."*

On November 10th they entered Mons. This morning of Monday, November 11 was cold and foggy, much as the weather of one year before at the battle of Cambai.

The previous evening at Mons, the Canadians had been waiting in strategic positions in the surrounding area. Fighting continued through the night, and at dawn the Canadian division entered the streets and established a line east of the town, while the carillons of the belfries played, *It's a Long Way to Tipperary,* Mons was both the last battle of World War I and for Emile's Canadian battalion. Armistice was signed Monday, November 11, 1918.

Awaiting the armistice, the officers gripped watches in their hands, and the troops demonstrated the same grave composure with which they had fought. Most men were too weary and deadened for their imaginations to rise to this great moment. It would be long afterward when they would finally grasp the vast drama of the four years of hell.

At two minutes to eleven, opposite the eastern most point reached by the British armies, a German machine gunner, fired off a belt without pause, stood beside his weapon, removed his helmet, bowed, and then walked slowly to the rear. Suddenly, as the watch-hands touched eleven, there came a second of expectant silence, and then a curious rippling sound that listeners far behind the front likened to the noise of a powerful wind. It was the sound of men cheering from the Vosges all the way to the sea. From this moment in Canadian history, came the expression of, *All's quiet on the Western Front*.

650,000 Canadians had served and 61,000 had died. In the last three months Canadian armies had gained seven victories, and had broken the heart of the enemy.

In hindsight, it would not be simplistic to say that the trench warfare of World War I was a massing of large numbers of soldiers unprotected by anything but cloth uniforms. However well they were trained, however well equipped, when they were pitted against large masses of other soldiers, protected only by earthworks and barbed wire and provided with rapid-fire weapons, it was bound to result in very heavy casualties. The effect of artillery added to the slaughter, as did that of bayonets and grenades when opposing troops came into close contact in the trench labyrinths.

The generalship of the First World War is one of the most controversial issues of its historiography. Good generals and bad generals abound in the millions of words written about this war and among the ranks of historians, so do critics and champions. In their time almost all the leading commanders of the war were seen as great men. But between the wars their reputations crumbled, with novelists relentlessly toppling the standing of those who had dominated from their former high perches. Both popular and academic historians continually portrayed generals as "donkeys leading lions," or even as psychological misfits leading a generation of innocent young men to their needless deaths.

It was a popular overview that the First World War exposed the oppressiveness of British class structure. The circumstances in which the war leaders lived were far removed from the cold rations, leaking beds, sodden uniforms, flooded trenches and plagues of lice, experienced by their troops. The leaders resided in distant sanitary and historic chateaus, with well-polished entourages, glittering automobiles and cavalry escorts, regular routines with sumptuous dinners, gala balls and uninterrupted hours of sleep. Infamous were the two-hour lunches, ten-hour nights, and champagne diets that were a world away from the realities of the battlefields.

The belief that the First World War exposed the oppressiveness of class structure links the two lives of Emile and Guillaume Pelletier, although the details maybe somewhat different. Just as all leaders in the seventeenth century were not irresponsible in sending lower classes out to the wilderness to create personal gain; many WWI generals also exposed themselves to risk. Thirty-four British generals were killed by artillery and twenty-two were killed by small-arms fire. However, the number is extremely low compared with ten million other human lives being lost, both military and civilian.

General Sir Arthur Currie, commander of the Canadian corps had forecast the cost of one of the assaults he led to be 16,000 casualties. At first he officially protested consigning his corps to this particular pointless sacrifice, but eventually complied with the orders from his superior, General Haig. The early winter had brought almost continuous rain, but the only way forward toward the top of the ridge his troops had to surmount was along two narrow causeways surrounded by bogs and streams. The ground was so wet that shells from their supporting artillery buried themselves in the mud without exploding. The cost to his four divisions of Canadian corps totaled 15,634 dead or seriously wounded, almost exactly the figure Currie had predicted. It was clear that war was a system; it clearly was not a system of human values.

Because of a lack of communication technology that was only a few years away, the World War I generals were like men without eyes, or ears or voices. They were unable to observe the operations they set in progress, unable to hear reports of new developments and unable to speak to those whom they had originally given orders once the action had begun. It would be the observations of the so-called lower classes, and not of the generals, that would survive as the singular aspect of humanity in all the atrocities of this war.

Emile Pelletier's diary continued after the armistice was signed:

"Rested in Havre' and Bonssoit till the 20th, then started this march to Germany. Through Belgium, through Manrage, Frevieres, Courcelles, Jumet, Kumice, Temploux, Namur, Bonneville, Nameche, Geneff, Heyd, Ottre, Beho. Crossed the German border from Beho to Krombach the 2nd of December. From Krombach through Manderfeld, Blackenheim, Arloff, Weidesheim, Endenich.

"Then entered Bonn, Germany, the 12th of December. Crossed the River Rhein, through Beuel to a place called Putzchen, where we were billeted in a school till the 24th of December. Then we left Putzchen for Vinxel where we were on outpost for six days. Then on the 30th we left for Beuel and this side of the river. Left for Belgium the 23rd of January. Reached Namur through Cologne and Liege by train the 24th. Marched eight kilos to Malonne. The 27th we left Malonne for Namur where we guarded canal boats for one week, then the 4th of February we came back to Malonne.

"Stayed there till the 27th of February when we went to Hug, Namieche and Namur. Came back then the 6th of March to Malonne, went to Brussels on leave the 22nd of March for sports held between the Canadians only. 31st is the football champions of the Canadian Corps. Visited the whole blooming place. Went to Overyessche where the 50th was, to see friends on the 23rd of March. Got back to Namur at 7:30. Left Maloune the 26th to join the 26th Battalion. Joined them that day in Famines about thirty kilos from Malonne in a lorrie. Left Famines the 5th of April at 12:30 for le Havre through Charleroi, Mons, Havre ville, Misseron, Arras, St. Pol, Doulens."

A war entirely subsidiary to the Great War ensued. In North Russia, a mixed French-British-American force, under the command of the formidable and physically gigantic British General Ironside, made well known the cause of the local anti-Bolshevik Social revolutionaries and pushed out a defensive perimeter with general cooperation of the commanders of the British intervention forces in the Baltic. Art Pelletier, Emile's older brother, had been stationed at this front.

In his later years, Art would tell of the devastation and hell - of Leningrad, later to be renamed St. Petersburg. Both he and his nephew, Lonnie Pelletier, held a great admiration for this great marble city, although their visits were one-half century apart, under completely different circumstance. Art was there in the heat and cries of battle, his nephew visited at leisure with an artistic tour group in the 1960's.

The long marches that Emile describes had a purpose. It appeared inevitable that Germany's political future would be settled by civil war in its capital and its provinces. The armies of the Allies were advancing to take possession of western Rhineland provinces and of the three bridgeheads across the river. At Mainz, Coblenz and Cologne the German army finally surrendered under the terms of armistice.

Emile returned to Canada with photographs that showed that the soldiers of the armies of occupation were quick to fraternize with the population. Antagonism was swiftly overlaid by friendships, all the more readily as army rations made their way from cook houses to family kitchens still subsisting on the meager wartime diet that the Allies' maintenance of a blockade had imposed. Hunger, even more than the threat of a full-scale invasion, was the measure that would eventually bring the German republic to sign the peace treaty on June 23, 1919.

The chronicle of the Great War's battles provides the dreariest literature in military history. There are no brave trumpets sounded in memory, and no litanies are sung for the leaders who coaxed millions to slaughter. Europe was temporarily ruined as a centre of world civilization. All that was uncivilized prevailed – the deliberate starvation of peasant enemies, the extermination of racial outcasts, persecution with intellectual and cultural objects of hate, the massacre of ethnic minorities, the extinction of small national sovereignties, the destruction of parliaments and the elevation of commissar and warlords to power over voiceless millions. All these had their origins in the chaos the war left behind. However, in a few short years, Europe would for the most part, restore itself to be prosperous, peaceful and powerful, existing for the good in the world. We as Canadians were a part of that positive process. Emile Pelletier had returned to his ancestor Guillaume's roots by playing a part as a pawn in a much larger international game, and he had risked his life and sacrificed to bring civilization in full circle.

* * *

Emile had watched his closest friends die at a time in history when the world was very naïve regarding the realities of the human mind and human emotions. The reality of post-traumatic stress disorder syndrome was not yet known. In fact it did not become a formal definition until after the Gulf War, at the end of this same century. After World War I, references to shell-shock were being made but they were not understood and could only be observed.

The fact that memory loss seems to plague fifty per cent of the survivors of long-term or repeated trauma is from recent studies within the last decade. A more complex theory was originally proposed in reference to war, family violence and sexual assault. It was postulated that people suffer memory loss of traumatic experiences because these incidents created moral or emotional conflicts for them. Killing others was an event that definitely created moral conflict. It was (and is) thought that the trauma was repressed because of the humiliation and shame involved.

Dissociative Systematized Amnesia was the disempowering ailment of post-traumatic stress disorder. Emile relied on his diary for the chronicle of his activities during World War I. After the war, when within social occasions, his entire reflection on his part in the First World War was that, "We marched a lot!" In part this was true. However, he had buried the reality of much of the terror. His diary in part explained his return:

*"Reached le Havre at 6 o'clock the 7th of April. Left the camp the 10th at 3:30 for the docks, got on and left at 6:30. Reached Southhampton at 1 o'clock on the 11th and landed at 8 o'clock. Left in a train for Wittey at 11, reached at 2. Went on leave from Wittey to London. Met Ferme Beck. Left London the same day, the 15th of April, for Nottingham. Left Nottingham for London the 23rd. Slept in the Union Jack Club. Left from Waterloo for Witty at 11:10. Reached Camp at 1 o'clock. Was there till the 2nd of May when I got leave till the 5th M.N.*

*"Visited the Zoo, St. Paul's Cathedral, the Wax Works, Westminster House of Parliament, Buckingham Palace. Was on the TRIUMPH MARCH through London of 12,000 troops. Canadians leading then, Australians, New Zealanders, South Africans, Newfoundlanders. Came back to camp at 1 pm the 6th.*

*"Then we left camp for Southampton at 8:30 the 10th of May. Left the station at 11 o'clock. Reached the boat (the Olympic) at 1 o'clock. Left Southampton at 8 o'clock and arrived at Halifax at 2 o'clock on Saturday the 16th.*

*"Landed at Halifax and took the train to St. John at 3 o'clock in the afternoon. Reached St. John at 6 pm. We had one hell of a big supper waiting for us! I got discharged at 10 pm on the 17th and was all dressed up in civies at 11 o'clock."*

This was a snapshot of the discharge period that Emile would often repeat. Many men and women returning from war have done the same. They would systematically recall, almost reverently, their friends of the time, recounting times spent in pubs, on dates and other off-duty pleasures. At the same time, at a conscious level at least, they would forget the horrors of war.

Upon returning to Canadian soil, Emile visited his many relatives in New Brunswick, before setting out for his new home in Western Canada. He had opted to be discharged in St. John for that purpose. In New Brunswick he was welcomed by the cousins, great aunts and great uncles of shared Pelletier ancestry.

His uncle Joe was now the High Sheriff and was a former member of the provincial Legislative Assembly. Emile was given the *royal tour* by his uncle and by his cousins. As he later recounted the events in the west, the pun was intended, as in this case, the high sheriff was directly appointed by the king and the position held specific social duties. This visit helped Emile come to terms with the apparent senselessness of the war; to experience his family's prosperity in Madawaska justified the pain and losses he had suffered to a certain extent. Protecting life back home, made a case for the few virtues of war, even in World War I.

A song that would become well known was very significant to Emile, even though it would not be popularized for a few more years. Entitled, "How're you going to keep them down on the farm, after they've seen Paris (Paree)," its lyrics reflect the dramatic culture shock Emile faced upon his return. He would be returning to Northern British Columbia backwoods. To consider coming back anything but a cultural shock would be to underestimate the lack of communication between the distant parts of Canada during the first two or three decades of the twentieth century.

Emile, therefore, had two issues with which to grapple. He would be required to live a quiet rural life and to present World War I in an acceptable manner, as a necessary war.

Patriotism was rampant, and most people who had not directly faced the war's horrors could only imagine its virtues. The returning veterans would oblige them. They would reminisce about the new friends, great experiences and far-off exotic lands. They would make it seem like a great adventure. Unfortunately they would inadvertently set the stage for a second great war just two decades later.

It had been said that, "men go to war because the women are watching." The quote is not entirely accurate, but that simplistic view of life in 1918 may still be gleaned from letters to Emile from his Aunt Edith. She had referred to "hoping he had good times", and "saluting his courage", then "marching through many of the old countries under the flag of Canada." These were all references to an imagined glory of war.

Other changes of mindset would evolve for many of the men of the old French-Canadian families. Being used as pawns within a hierarchy, as in a giant chess game, had an historical familiarity to it. Statements in referring to the Pelletier family ancestors as having served under "a very good seigneur" were now too obvious as a paradox. An acceptance of feudal control could no longer exist.

Emile and his comrades in arms could also no longer accept the controls and restrictions of seventeenth-century religion. Blind obedience to the church would never be replicated after World War I; they had lived the consequences. Emile no longer could relate to relationships between men and women as the Church had presented them in the eighteenth century. For example, he could no longer accept women as mere baby factories for the glory of king and country. Experiencing life, death and other cultures allows anyone to look upon their own culture with a more severe judgment.

Speaking out about these issues would soon follow for Canadian society in general. The new post-war mentality began sweeping throughout French-speaking Canada, and empathy for the struggles of womanhood would now be the norm.

Some of the glories of war, did exist and they were valid. Honours were bestowed with respect and they were graciously received. In 1919, King George V approved the British War Medal. Its purpose was to record the conclusion of the war and honour the services rendered by His Majesty's Forces. Emile received two medals and two "mentions in dispatches".

One medal, which hangs from its ribbon by a straight clasp, without swivel, bears on the obverse the effigy of His Majesty with the legend, Georgivs V Britt: Omn: Rex Et Ind: Imp. The reverse depicts St. George on horseback trampling underfoot the eagle shield of the Central Powers and skull and crossbones, the emblem of death. Above, between the horse's neck and the knee of the rider, is the risen sun of Victory. The naked male figure, rather than a more typical symbolical female one, was chosen because men had borne the brunt of the fighting. The figure was mounted on horseback as symbolic of man's mind controlling a force - represented by the horse - of greater strength than his own. The short sword is an allegory of the physical and mental strength that achieves victory over Prussianism. Prussianism was then defined as a harsh military discipline lacking freedom. The design was also symbolic of the mechanical and scientific appliances that had helped to win. The ribbon has an orange watered centre with stripes of white and black on each side, with borders of royal blue. A total of 427,933 Canadians. living and killed, were issued this medal.

A second honour awarded to Emile Pelletier was the British Victory Medal, authorized in 1919. It was also known as the Inter-Allied War Medal. This medal is circular and is of copper lacquered bronze. It bears on the obverse a winged full-length figure of Victory with her left arm extended and holding a palm branch in her right hand. On the reverse is the inscription, "The Great War For Civilization," with a line of dots below the words surrounded by a wreath. The rim is plain, and the medal hangs from a ring. The ribbon is red in the centre, with green and violet on either side shaded to form the colours of two rainbows - violet-blue-green-yellow-orange centre.

It was further approved that any officer or man who had been, "mentioned in dispatches" should wear a small bronze oak-leaf pin on the ribbon of this medal. The oakleaf was issued in two sizes. The larger, worn with the medal, was affixed to the centre of the ribbon at an angle of sixty degrees from the inside edge of the ribbon, stem to the right. The smaller was worn, when the wearer was in service dress. Emile Pelletier was awarded both of these two bronze oak-leaf pins.

Both battling sides had attempted the use of airplanes, but they were still too flimsy to be effective. Poison gas was tried, but as Emile had later described from personal experience, "it was quickly discovered that a shift in wind brought the gas back onto their initiating line and troops." Tanks were used but they were too few in number, and then too prone to break down. The great weapons of trench warfare were the repeating rifle, the machine gun, and the fast-firing artillery pieces.

Like many of his fellow soldiers from the Great War, Emile would never forget the fact that more than sixty thousand Canadians did not return. Of those Canadian men, who had enlisted, one in eleven was killed. Many thousands more men were wounded seriously.

Emile's only physical scar was on his big toe. Shrapnel, from the explosion of a bomb in the trenches, had damaged it extensively. However, Emile grew accustomed to shrugging it off, and it became a humorous one-liner. If asked about the Great War, Emile would often ask if the person wanting to discuss it, wanted to see his big toe. In social settings the comment became a great ice-breaker.

Among Emile's personal effects, like other doughboys, he had carried a miniature war manual along with his diary. Battalions were defined as the administrative unit of infantry, consisting of headquarters, four companies and a machine gun section. The same manual included "aeronautical terms". Listed were definitions of an: "Aeroplane, Aviator, Biplane, Monoplane, and Nacelle" (as the car of a balloon or dirigible). However, the manual's main focus was on other terms - this was the war where "Flying Balloon Terms," and "Horses and their Care" were a much larger and more important section. This had truly been a manual war.

# Chapter 11 - Western Lumbermen

Stanley Pelletier had moved his family to Western Canada from St. Francois, New Brunswick, in 1901. He established a new Pelletier Lumber Mill between the towns of Coleman and Blairmore in the foothills of the Rocky Mountains, in the area that would soon become the province of Alberta. After the 1885 Northwest Rebellion, peace had been restored; and the Crowsnest Canadian Pacific Railway, the Kootenay Railway and the Alberta Rail lines were now in operation. This was still the somewhat wild west of the Northwest Territories.

Lumbering had been Canada's biggest industry during the last half of the nineteenth century. In both this area and in the east, trees were felled in winter when logs could be skidded along frozen ground. The men who felled and squared the logs also shepherded them along the river or lake drives to the mill. The hardy loggers worked in pairs, taking alternative swings at the tree. The Pelletiers had used oxen in Eastern Canada for the hauling and dragging logs to the lake or river's edge. However, here they used mules and horses, pulling out each log, one at a time. The logs were then stacked for a spring drive, and when the ice broke, they were herded down the river or stream or across the lake, to the railway yard. It was the existence of rail that allowed Stanley, and later his brother George Pelletier, to open new mills in the West.

However, after the Frank Slide of April 29, 1903, close to their home, the family returned to New Brunswick for a brief time. Scattered rocks thirty meters deep cover three-square kilometres of the valley of the Oldman River in gruesome testimony to the Frank Slide. That day at 4:10 a.m., a wedge of limestone mountain 915 metres wide, 640 metres high, and 150 metres thick. hurled down the side of Turtle Mountain toward the sleeping town of Frank.

After one minute and forty seconds, some 82 million tonnes of rock was strewn across the valley floor. Seventy people died, and part of the town- including a mine plant and a railway siding- had disappeared. Geologists believe the slide was caused by a mild earthquake that had passed through the area earlier in 1901. After the slide a new town began to grow nearby. Blairmore is two kilometres from the slide. Coleman is 8.5 kilometres away. The Pelletier home was in between, just barely set away from this great rumble and roar of 1903. From that day forward, Stanley's wife Edith, shaken and frightened, counted the days until she could return to the east. However, it was not only Edith's wish to relocate the family that caused the decision to move back east as schooling would now become important to the children.

Spruce, poplar and lodgepole pine are the indigenous species of trees found in this area. The lodgepole pine was used for both railway ties and mine props or beams. Both a coal mining area and a railway cross through, prior to 1903, the town of Frank had provided Stanley Pelletier with a lumber market for both. After the slide Stanley's lumber business diminished considerably. With a good deal of sadness, they sold the faltering mill and returned to Eastern Canada.

After the loss of his wife in New Brunswick in 1909, Stanley felt he needed a more stable future and better opportunities for his children. Returning to the West, Stanley began operating a sawmill farther out of town at Hammy, Alberta, and then in 1914 he moved his sawmill back to close to Coleman, Alberta. Here Stanley opened the sawmill in the shadow of the always-handsome Crowsnest Mountain.

In the Crowsnest Pass, an area of wild-west history, the wind sometimes reaches 160 kilometres an hour and has been known to push boxcars on the railway as fast as 24 kilometers an hour. In the tradition of folklore, old-timers told of a wind-measuring device that was made up of a large steel ball suspended by a chain from a high pole. When the ball and chain pointed straight out, it was said locals could figure that there was a "fair wind."

The Pelletier home here was typical of the area and period. It was built as one large room, divided by a pot-bellied stove and a large wood stove at its center, with living and dining areas on either side. The cabin was always cozy and warm in the central kitchen area near the stoves. The winters were long with the single pane windows iced much of the time. Floors were constructed of planks that needed to be continually washed. The ceiling rafters matched Stanley's six-foot stature - he needed to duck between them in moving about. Beside the entry door was the all-important wood box providing fuel for critical warmth from the cold winter winds.

Two lean-to rooms were built off the main room for bedroom use. A steep stairway on the side of the main room led to one large attic bedroom with a window at each end that provided most of its light. This was a time of oil lamps and sleeping and rising with the sun. A loaded hunting rifle always hung above the entry door to the home. It was necessary to be on constant guard against overly hungry wolves and unusually aggressive bears.

A barn was always needed; as horses were not a luxury and required stabling. Automobiles, a definite luxury, were not to be relied on in deep snows. In this still untamed West, men and even women carried rifles for their protection. For another fifty years in the foothills of Western Canada it was not unusual to see a rifle mounted above the back window of a pick-up truck. At the turn of the century it was the trailing packhorse that would carry a rifle, if the horse ridden didn't. Anyone carrying a pistol in plain view, however, was unacceptable. A community pride in being more civilized than "those southerners" had evolved. This was never the American West, even before the turn of the century.

On the outskirts of Coleman is Crowsnest Lake, where an entire train, complete with box cars and caboose, lies at the lake bottom. It plunged into the icy depths during the period in which Stanley Pelletier and his family lived in Coleman. The train, carrying illicit whisky during prohibition, had left the track after the engineer had sampled too much of his cargo. Neither the whisky nor the train was ever recovered. During years between 1916 and 1919 many individuals of this raw land were involved with the economic alternative of smuggling alcohol across the nearby American border.

Stanley greeted the move to northern British Columbia, *Peace River Country,* with great enthusiasm. Land was inexpensive, in plentiful supply, and of extremely rich soil. He arrived in the Dawson Creek area in 1918 and took on the challenge of a quarter-section homestead in the South Dawson district. His two sons, Art and Emile, joined him upon their return from the war. As soon as he had completed the construction of his large home, the younger children, Jeff, Yvonne and Albertine, had joined him.

Eva, having been raised by Stanley's brother George and his sister-in-law Edith, rejoined her immediate family when George and Edith were to move to Dawson Creek in 1926. George and Fred Pelletier had operated a sawmill at Prince Rupert until they joined their families in the Dawson Creek area. Stanley and Emile would both work at their new sawmill along with working their own South Dawson farms. George would carry on the three-generation family tradition of lumber mill operation and work, until his death in 1937.

Some individuals who had worked at Pelletier Mill, New Brunswick also moved with Stanley from the Blairmore, Hammy and Coleman areas. Discontented with the economy of these areas, and having heard great reports of life in the Peace River Country, they would now follow their dreams with the goal of owning land. They all achieved that goal.

A number of them recounted in later years how they were welcomed. "Upon arriving, being graciously accepted into Stanley Pelletier's large home such that we could then get established." In the book "Lure of the South Peace", tribute is paid to Stanley for this hospitality in sharing his two-storey home. Two generations later these families who would make this specific reference, in tribute to Stanley for his generosity.

Stanley and his two sons now owned farms within one kilometer of one another in the South Dawson valley. The town was moved to the location to be known as Dawson Creek, and South Dawson remained agricultural. It was a beautiful region of rolling hills, gently sloping fields, and had a significant resemblance to St. Francois, New Brunswick. Both areas were a mix of farms and lumber mills – and both were home.

Stanley's South Dawson home was the style of a stately French-Canadian house. Its ground floor was above ground on a rock foundation built with shiplap siding. It had a steeply pitched roof with a large overhang, and hipped dormer windows. The windows and doors were symmetrically spaced. Stanley had purchased a doorway in New Brunswick through his brother Joe, and with pride he could mention that it had survived the journey. For accent he added eclectic touches of decorated window and door frames. Along with the dormer windows and peaked roof, the most obvious difference between this home and others of this area and time was the large front veranda.

Stanley was also involved in the founding of a cooperative store, allowing this far northern community to obtain access to general goods. Dawson Creek was a few days travel by car from the nearest city of Edmonton, Alberta. The store's original location had been at South Dawson, a few miles closer to the Pelletier farm. In 1930 and 1931, Stanley was involved in the moving of the entire town- with all of its buildings. It had been in a dead end valley and as such, the town needed moving so the railroad could make its turnaround, as a terminus. The enormous undertaking was achieved only through "great cooperation of community and horses."

Between the provincial capital in the south of B.C. and the Peace River Block area, it had always been said that, "you can't get there from here." The only road was single lane mud, stretching from Edmonton, Alberta. The Alaska Highway to the north would be built a number of years later in 1942.

Stanley Pelletier died April 13, 1939 at seventy-two years of age. He had suffered a stroke on April 2nd, and was taken to the hospital the following day. A funeral procession, the largest ever seen locally, left from the home on 3rd Avenue, of his son Art, and proceeded to the Catholic church, where high mass was sung. This was followed by a heavily attended funeral burial in the local Catholic cemetery.

# THE SUBTLE COMIC

The legal process of the Great War's armistice called for bilingual interpreters, and Emile Pelletier became involved as a French/English translator. At that time, the translation department of the federal government did not exist. Rather, in one of many groups formed, Emile Pelletier and six of his colleagues were chosen from the army. He sent a postcard to his younger sister, Eva from Ostend, Belgium, where he briefly worked. On it, Emile wrote enthusiastically of his private room and that his hotel "had a bathroom on every floor!" He considered this to be his reward for receiving a bilingual New Brunswick education.

After his involvement in the Great War, Emile joined his father Stanley in northern British Columbia. Emile was immediately able to take up a second quarter-section homestead adjoining his father's in South Dawson, in a beautiful and quiet valley setting.

A favourite story, because it captured the spirit of the Canadian North and the essence of north-country humour, is a tale from the first summer that Emile rather reluctantly settled in following his return from Europe.

From 1916 to the late twenties, there had existed a prohibition on alcoholic beverages, and Emile, as it was often stated, "made very good rum." Because of his creativity, which was not appreciated by the local police, he was charged, convicted and sentenced. Making one's own liquor was a popular local custom; however, getting caught was decidedly not. Homemade spirits were especially popular in the Crowsnest Pass area, from where he had recently moved. During this period the small towns throughout northwestern Canada were, on average, one hundred miles apart. Most of the northern population felt they should be exempt from such southern laws as prohibition.

At that time the police who patrolled this vast area made a practice of putting the criminals to work. It was decreed by a Sergeant Duncan, both magistrate and police officer, that Emile would be incarcerated and that he would have a number of duties to perform. They included sawing logs for the police office firewood and planting a large garden at the government building in the nearby village of Pouce Coupe.

Emile cheerfully carried out his given tasks. He worked hard at cutting the year's supply of logs out of a huge pile of wood. The logs were precisely cut to the same length. He was, after all, a carpenter and he had worked for his father as a millwright. He also took great care in planting the garden. The garden rows were planted with meticulous attention. Because of his unique effort and dedication, Emile soon was given a leave from further duties and the balance of the detention time. It would be said often that Sergeant Duncan thanked him with great enthusiasm.

Weeks later when the harvest winds began to blow, as the story goes, the truth was slowly revealed. The seeds, had not in fact, been planted, but had been left at the end of each perfect row, buried in one small mound. As this winter's cold appeared, the size of the pot bellied stove was found to be somewhat inadequate for the huge pile of firewood. All of the precisely cut wood had been cut exactly two inches too long for this type of stove.

This kind of tale had been very much a part of both Acadia and early Canadian enjoyment. Delight in life as it was, was the paramount focus.

Emile Pelletier married Yvonne Roberts on September 23, 1940. Yvonne Marcia Roberts was born November 14, 1920 at Oaks, North Dakota, USA. She later divorced Emile and married a drifter named Buzz. Their only son, Lonnie, was to remain with the rather irresponsible two; changing schools eleven times by the age of eleven.

In 1942 construction of the Alaska Highway brought 16,000 men from the United States army, plus many civilians through Dawson Creek. An entire regiment of U.S. Army Engineers suddenly appeared at the tiny settlement. In order to capitalize on the boom, Emile organized a taxi business called *Mile Zero Cab Company*. Dawson Creek was the starting point of this rough road through the north, which at 1900 kilometres was labeled "the longest highway in the world." The main army base was on the outskirts of town, and with the only liquor store eleven kilometres away in the small town of Pouce Coupe, the taxi service became lucrative. Constant trips adding up to hundreds of fares enabled Emile to do exceptionally well financially. Emile endured World War II with much more dignity than he had the First World War. He also was able to graciously give jobs to several of his wife's brothers, driving cab when they were home on leave from three armed forces and their numerous locations.

Over the following years Emile worked as both a carpenter and construction superintendent on many schools, auditoriums and government buildings. He also usually owned a horse, as by character and tradition, he and his family were horsemen. Raising and breaking horses would become a way of life carried on by the following generation in the Dawson Creek area. For this reason alone, Emile held onto his quarter-section farm, even after acquiring various real estate properties in Dawson Creek.

Emile Pelletier died on March 14, 1955 at fifty-six years of age, in Dawson Creek, BC, while living at the farm of his brother Jeff Pelletier. He died of an ailment common to those who had hardening of the arteries, due to the unfortunate bachelor oriented eating habits of the day.

Back in New Brunswick, in 1949, a coat of arms for the republic of Madawaska was created. The publicity value and historical quirk of a republic existing within the heart of a constitutional monarchy was attractive to the tourist industry. Edmundston, New Brunswick became the republic's capital, and an official flag was also designed. The flag featured a bald eagle as a symbol of Madawaska's independent spirit. Six red stars represent the republic's cultural groups. They are native Indian, Acadian, French Canadian, English, American and Irish. The republic's own French dialect is known as Brayon. It was the spirit of the ancestors of Emile Pelletier that were being honoured. However, although he was proud of being

French-Canadian, Western Canadian and of Acadian ancestry, Emile could not relate patriotically to his former county of Madawaska. He had become too far removed and his dialect definitely had not evolved into being the local *Brayon*.

\* \* \*

Denis "Jeff" Pelletier was the youngest member of the Pelletier family in Western Canada. It seemed that his nickname had always been Jeff. With teasing older brothers like Art and Emile, it would have been unusual if he hadn't been given a nickname. As in most added names, even after his death it would seem unusual to refer to him as Denis.

After moving to the Dawson Creek, British Columbia area, Jeff started a wagon and freight service using mules to haul trade goods and Hudson Bay Company freight from Dawson Creek,-through and over the pass to the Pine Valley, ending at Moberly Lake. He would follow the banks of East Pine River Bank as a trail as it wound through the mountain range with his mules. They were more surefooted than horses for this type of work. With his partner Bud Lineham, who would later become his brother-in-law, he operated a four-horse team. This was a classic wagon freight route; along its path the general store owners would welcome Jeff and Bud's shouts as they neared the secluded mountain homes. This customary greeting truly evoked the presence of the *couriers de bois spirit* of past centuries in Canada. It was as if the pioneers of yesteryear had just rounded the bend in the river in their canoes, nearing the village docks. Their wagon train shouts announcing their arrival in a rural community could not have been more traditional than those of earlier canoeing times in Canada.

Jeff homesteaded seven miles west of Dawson Creek in South Dawson, one-half mile away from Stanley Pelletier's farm. His home was a picturesque cabin, well built in the style of squared log construction. Its corner logs were dovetailed and its doors and windows were handmade. His driveway wound around and into his cabin and the creek behind skirted tall pines. For years he enjoyed stating as if it were a fact of history. "I guess I should let you know that I am responsible for the start of Dawson Creek." He would pause for effect and then continue, "My farm is at the headwater – I have pigs. It begins with a trickle. If you want to see how Dawson Creek starts, just visit my pig pen."

Other creatures - wildlife, deer, moose and smaller animals - would continually visit his front porch, where he left salt out for them. Wildfowl constantly fed at the side of his cabin, as he had planned. His was the life of a bachelor homesteader and by all accounts he seemed to enjoy it.

Four hundred years had passed between the family's coal merchant roots in France and establishing themselves as Western Canadians. More than anything else, being Western Canadian meant one thing– freedom– freedom to decide occupation, level of education, level of entrepreneurial challenge, and the amount of real estate owned.

On a social level as well, much of the world had changed. People were no longer officially labeled by occupation or status in the community. At this juncture in the chronicles of the Pelletier family, there can be a pause for reflection upon entrepreneurial spirit – no more extraordinary than thousands of other immigrants who made Canada their new home.

*C'est ca - enfin là mode de vie de libre arbitre.* Or translated: "That's it – finally a lifestyle of free will."

# PELLETIER CHRONICLES - 500 YEARS

## PART II
## My personal Involvement

# PART II - My personal involvement

## Chapter 12 - The Journey of Time

### THE AUTHOR

My name is Lonnie Pelletier. I was born January 7, 1943 in Dawson Creek, B.C. I married, was blessed with two wonderful children and have lived near the Pacific Ocean of Canada for most of my life.

I grew up in poverty under the same roof as the man who was the second husband of my mother, Yvonne Marcia Roberts Pelletier Lawson. My father Emile Pelletier died as I turned twelve. My parents had been separated and divorced since I was six. I was never fully accepted into the rather reckless and irresponsible Lawson family, nor was I legally adopted so I never considered myself one of them. Throughout my youth I was able to retain a pride in my Pelletier heritage.

Undoubtedly because of my fragmented childhood, I have always felt a great empathy for individuals who did not know their parents, or their heritage. My aspirations, achievements, relationships and family values were predicated upon my understanding of the dignity of my own family history. My heritage was – and still is – a part of my *raisond'être*.

For many years I was successful within the industry of real estate. As I approached the age of sixty, however, I realized it was time to follow my passions - back into the world of the Arts. One of the tasks I set for myself was to gather together everything I understood about my heritage, and put pen to paper. I also understood that it was important to analyze what being a Canadian meant. Before I did anything else, I knew I needed to visit my family's history at its sources: France, Quebec, and New Brunswick.

It is normal for a Western Canadian to have travelled the world, yet never to have visited Eastern Canada. The same is true of Eastern Canadians. I have visited forty-five countries, including all the continents except Australia and Antarctica, yet before 2004, I had never been east of Quebec City. It now seemed imperative to put Eastern Canada on my list of places to visit.

By 2004, I had already put part of my plan to follow my artistic dreams into action: I had become a professional painter. My passion and art training acquired in the Paris of the 1960s, could still be utilized. This would serve me well as I traveled across Canada's vast and varied terrain, as I would paint landscapes along my journey. This blending of artistic expression with the discovery of my heritage seemed a beautiful synchronicity to me. It was about time for me to place myself squarely within that lineage.

My journey would include the sites where my ancestors housed, fed and clothed their families, nurturing their souls and minds through hardships, learning to enjoy the simple pleasures their lives afforded. I had traveled by car through nine of the provinces of this great land and upon arriving in Nova Scotia, I was convinced that every Canadian should make this road trip. Only in this manner is it possible to feel Canada's vastness and witness her visual splendor. I also found that, in exploring the roads and backroads in this way, any cultural differences seemed non-existent. As I crossed provincial lines, each border occupations mirrored themselves. Waitresses, gas station attendants, middle managers, museum curators - everyone had a counterpart in each of the other provinces. Few cultural differences existed - we are truly one culture. In this observation I include not only French-speaking and English-speaking Canadians, but also the dozens of other ethnic minorities Canada has welcomed. When I did venture south across the American border, I immediately perceived distinct differences.

I made a fortuitous decision to travel through northern Ontario, and rural Quebec, and I was not disappointed. The warmth and friendliness of the people in these small towns was akin to what I had felt in northern British Columbia and Alberta. It may be the case that, as a group, the inhabitants of Canada's largest cities have distinct personalities and character traits; however mine was a rural, *blue jeans* kind of a trip. I wanted to know the Canada my ancestors had known: that of small town camaraderie and shared community spirit.

I had driven through the Canadian Rockies and had crossed the Prairies on many previous occasions; this time I would link Ontario and the Canadian Shield. As a longtime admirer of the artists of the Group of Seven I took pleasure in camping at parks on the north shore of Lake Superior. As many others had done, I was able to relive the aesthetic quests of Lawren Harris and A. Y. Jackson. Camping in Algonquin Park while comparing Tom Thompson's landscapes in my memory was also an achievement. Mostly I was able to realize that I had grown up in a similar place. Several weeks later and hundreds of miles east, I was surprised to find I had the very same feelings about the Maritimes.

But I didn't identify with Prince Edward Island as a place like home. I have never lived on a potato farm. Agricultural fields joining the sea offered the closest thing to culture shock that I would experience. In visiting the Island, I suspected that I was one of millions who, although they enjoyed visiting, knew they could never make it their home.

As a painter of ocean scenes and historic ships, I spent a day with the curator of the County Museum, in Yarmouth, Nova Scotia. We shared our enjoyment of Yarmouth's Golden Age of Sail, on canvasses too numerous to list. I was given a personal tour of all of the paintings in the museum's archive. We two men from opposite oceans, yet from the same country had very much in common.

\* \* \*

My tour through time was about more than merely finding family ties and ancestral destinations. It was also about finding Canada. Instinctively, I knew that understanding my surroundings would allow me to better understand myself. I also knew I had vast ground to cover: my surroundings comprised an entire country and four hundred years of history. Guillaume and Emile Pelletier had introduced me to that quest and that experience.

During my journey to the place of my ancestry in Eastern Canada, I had looked forward to many new experiences. For one thing, I had planned on venturing to the eastern shores to enjoy the view of an iceberg flowing to the south. I didn't see one. It was both the wrong time of year and at a latitude too far south for the experience. I didn't see my ancestors either, but I had hoped that I would at least feel their presence, and I think I did.

For my ancestors faith was held as supreme. The joys of their relationships were not to be ended on earth by parting or death, but rather would be recreated at a final destination and that other kingdom. Their world of disease, pain, and suffering- and often an early death- was so prevalent as to be unconsciously present at all times. In centuries past a focus existed on life as a proving ground on earth with tears, for a people destined for what they hoped was the bliss of a better world in an eternal heaven.

Even the existence of justice was considered to be addressed to God, as good would be rewarded and evil would be punished. It contributed to a stagnant social order amongst them with little thought of the need for reform. They were taught to accept and live within their family's social status into which they had been born, as mere pawns in a chess game. The imagined heavenly reward for the righteous or the dreaded punishment, pending in the pits of hell, was so intense that it was a prime focus of daily living. As Catholics, they believed that the intermediate state of purgatory filled the gap between those destined for heaven and those destined for hell. This became a motivator for their behavior. To shorten one's time in purgatory before one entered heaven and the realm of eternal bliss was not an insignificant desire. As such it was a specific goal. A strong church combined with dictatorial government preyed on these fears and used them as a controlling force. Leaving France and living in Canada gave some relief from this overbearing control.

In the years prior to the twentieth century, it was the lack of individual rights that created the dichotomy of hollow praise mixed with confessions of unworthiness - accompanied by pleas for mercy- all within a stratified class system. All of this religious dogma was directly connected to government, a fact that is almost beyond modern day perceptions.

I am not attempting to make an individual statement about a specific belief in life everlasting, but only to present an alternative thought – the thought that these pioneers still live on! Our ancestors and those of us who are their offspring will live through our own children. We also live through our friends and our associates in a powerful way. We carry with us the heritage of a gene pool that created us, and we are of a cultural and emotional history that shaped us. We often list – in detail -our family traits as ideal qualities. They are like inner demands that drive us to survival and often times to achievement.

We also achieve a level of immortality through our relationships and personal associations. Our ancestors shared their historic tales with other family members and friends. Many of these forged relationships will remain forever unknown; nevertheless the thought patterns they engendered live on flying in an eternal wind. There is immortality in the passing on of thoughts, ideas and intense emotions.

As a parent and grandparent, I am now the one who will get to live on in the imaginations of my offspring. In that there is eternity for all of the family, in the past, present and future.

\* \* \*

In June 2005, I left Vancouver, BC, on my cross-country odyssey- a trip from the Pacific shores to the Atlantic's. I knew my route, but I arrived in the province of Quebec uncertain to what emotion I might feel. I was attempting to follow and if possible feel the warm emotions of my family roots. The site of the Pelletier family's first home at Beauport, was exactly 5,500 kilometres from the Pacific Ocean shore of my own home.

It was beyond my imagination that I would later feel that I was a French-Canadian. As usual, during my travels to the east I had begun to fear speaking French again. It had been a few years since I had used the language. Then, as I checked into the *Motel des Berges*, the proprietor simply ignored my request of English being used, which was perfect. Just those few simple sentences had inspired me to begin to think in French again. This was the Côte-de-Beupré, visited by millions each year, and it seemed that he did not want to tarnish its pervading French character. I didn't blame him. At this point; however, I didn't yet feel that it was my family's former home. Historical fact had not yet planted that emotional seed.

I began by visiting the archival library of Chateâu-Richer. I learned that in Quebec each village has a centre of genealogy that promotes ancestral pride along with restoring and preserving antique documents. The staff was helpful in letting me know what I could expect to find both here and on the Island of Orleans. The Guillaume Pelletier farm was not shown on the legal map of the area with his name; as the two existing maps only showed the original habitations. The Pelletiers' occupancy and registration was three years after the original purchase of those rights.

Now only a few minutes' drive from Quebec City, Parc de la Chute-Montmorency is a beautiful park, entirely removed from the hostile setting of the seventeenth century. The falls are 83 metres high, making them 30 metres higher than Niagara Falls. An elaborate hotel was built on the site in 1901 and the setting is one of summer theatre, terraced cafés and a geological interpretation centre.

The park's boundary overlaps the eastern perimeter of the farm owned by Antoine Pelletier. Guillaume's farm abutted Antoine's to the northwest. It was here that I had planned to stand and marvel at the first farm of the Pelletier family in Canada of September 12, 1644. As hundreds of the Pelletier families have done before and possibly since, I slowly walked the farm area. My intention was to remain philosophical; this was the first site on which my ancestors had also trod. However, as the diesel buses roared by, it was difficult to be overly nostalgic. I could have gotten run over. As a residential area it is now busy, as an intersection with winding feeder roads used by busy drivers. Their last thoughts would be envisioning plowing slowly through with oxen.

I now felt compelled to follow the tourist route *de la Nouvelle-France* in these suburbs. My next visit was to *La Petite Ferme* and *Le Moulin du Petit Pré*. Champlain initially established *La Petite Ferme* in 1626; *La Grande Ferme* was created later in 1640 under Laval. As I traipsed through the area, I mused that this was where Guillaume Pelletier most likely would have toiled for the Seigneur Giffard. It is probable that he and his brother Antoine were hired as woodworkers here.

I now again paused and stood quietly observing the hills and trees. The buildings had been restored to the point of near-newness. It was terrain that my ancestors would have known and we could share this viewpoint of observation. The next logical step was to drive the rest of this route and enjoy the architecture that is so specifically of Quebec and another place in time.

As I left this *route de la Nouvelle-France*, to cross the bridge to Îsle d'Orléans I felt that I was leaving Guillaume Pelletier behind. My feeling of needing to say adieu was offset by the fact that I would return to his world at a later date - in France. My intention was to visit his birthplace in 2005, in Bresolettes.

In 1663, Jean Pelletier took over an existing farm from Jean and Nicolas Juchereau, two brothers who enjoyed adventure more than toiling the land. It was equivalent to 116.94 square metres and it was situated from the middle of the island to the St. Lawrence River. By 1667, he had purchased two neighbouring properties, tripling his land holdings, which worked out to be approximately 3.5 hectares. Due to its size, and the hardship of island life, it is understandable that Jean would sell this farm on Île D'Orléans and move back to the mainland. His next ownership was on the south bank at St. Roch des Aulnaies.

Jean was nicknamed *Le Gobloteux* as was shown on the land use title. He loved to make ceramic goblets. None have survived, but this passion tells us that his thinking included a world outside of farming. Artistic flair was valued in the New World at that time. Unfortunately, it wasn't respected to the point of high remuneration.

I visited the island by way of a paved circle road. Old buildings from the eighteenth century were open to the public as museums. As I explored them, I attempted to mentally create a vision of life here in the late seventeenth century.

Armed with the new municipal address of 695-697 Chemin Royal, I now felt ready to visit the farm site. The duplex on the site was set off to one side. The relatively new building on this ancient farm was a classic in its own sense. It was built in the 1950s when most people had completely abandoned the outward form of the traditional rural Quebec house. Gone was the steep roof with a ridge that ran parallel to the road. Such a home was the symbol of Quebec and was precious to both landscape artists and antiquarians. However newer architectural ideas had created square boxes with a nearly flat roof, as this home possessed. The newer form allows more room upstairs and is obviously better suited for apartments. Such box-shaped houses, which became predominant in many regions, are often decorated with ornate false fronts and cornices. As was done across Canada, the owner would occasionally stucco his house and insert glittering colored glass in the stucco. Large picture windows and even large kitchens became the norm. The kitchen was the warmest point of the house, and therefore the focal point. The homes built in the 1950s on Île D'Orléans, were a style several steps removed from the traditional and quaint styles that had survived.

The paved main road ran through the centre of the former property. It was a beautiful summer day and I enjoyed the moment. While taking a few photographs, I walked out on the properties and again contemplated the horizon. The view of the St. Lawrence River below and the surrounding agricultural land could not have changed much in several hundred years. This was my second attempt at understanding the place, but not the time of my ancestors. It felt good to stand in the centre of this field, however the difference of it being a few minutes, or a few hours stop on the site, didn't seem to be significant. Just as Jean and his family had done over three hundred years earlier – I finally left for the south bank. Unlike my ancestors, I used the modern bridge and a six-lane highway for that part of the journey.

I arrived on the south bank in late evening, just in time to book into a local hotel. According to its brochure, the town of only a few hundred people had a major museum. The next morning, I visited the Musée Maritime du Quebec, and it was here that I discovered my real quest. I was focused on finding my family roots – the real ones – not the false ones of a same family name. Although large, it did not contain any trace of my authentic lineage. I left after only a few hours of enjoying many seafaring exhibits – my secondary passion.

Arriving in St.-Roch-des-Aulnaies I was mentally prepared to begin a difficult search for the locations of four generations of my family. What actually happened took less than a couple of hours in total. As I approached the town, a huge church loomed on the horizon. It appeared old, perhaps gothic, and my hopes were high- I knew that the fourth generation of my family here had built a church. However, as I approached the parking lot, I could readily see that this was a nineteenth century church and I continued through the town. To my left and almost on the edge of the highway - which was now the main street - was a small chapel. Built out of stone, it looked ancient and regal.

It was irresistible; I parked and entered. Interestingly, perhaps from a philosophical perspective, Quebec churches are often left open. In Western Canada they are locked during the week. This was the Chapel Notre Dame de Lourdes. Inside this one room building was the inscription that I was looking for.

The inscription reads: *Les paroissiens auraient fourni la pierre et le bois, mais sa réalisation est largement due à la générosite de Jean-Baptist Pelletier, citoyen de St.-Roch et député du comté L'Islet au Parlement canadien...*

In English, simply put, it thanked Jean-Baptiste Pelletier for building the church in 1792. I paused there for an hour, taking photos and reveling in my history. I had built a Lutheran church on the Pacific coast in1986: the country was beginning to feel much smaller. Even though the church I had spent one year building was "mainstream protestant", the similarities, between myself and my church-building family of two hundred years ago were very much in evidence. Devotion to community was a constant norm.

Next I needed to look for the farm. In Eastern Canada, when a street is named after a family, there is a high probability that the name is of the original pioneering family farm. In such a small town it was easy to find rue Pelletier. Part of the original farm was now a municipal park, so it was also easy to relax and contemplate this third family location. Jean Pelletier had chosen a beautiful site. And the farm ran gently into the St. Lawrence river.

Jean's son Charles with Marie-Barbe lived here from 1711 to 1748. Charles's son Pierre Pelletier was born here in 1731 and he then lived here until 1757. Charles's grandson, Jean-Baptiste Pelletier was born later in Kamouraska, however he would return to St.-Roch-des-Aulnaies to build the chapel. Jean-Baptiste subsequently married Madeline Pellerin in that same church. I had a marvelous time of contemplation and reflection at both the church and the farmsite. After a time though there was nothing else left but to continue on.

I had no particular plan in mind as I was headed toward the next Pelletier farm. I stopped at La Seigneurie des Aulnaies. A museum of former life in Saint-Roch-des-Aulnaies, the visit seemed to fit perfectly with the day. I had been told about a Pelletier family monument but I hadn't yet determined where it was. As I pulled into the parking lot, I immediately viewed two monuments, both just off to the side and both with a picturesque backdrop of flowers and shrubberies. One was emblazoned with the Pelletier family crest with "Les Pelletier" and the logo of "Stella Ducet" inscribed on two lines beneath. The body of the text is as follows as translated from French to English:

> *"The Pelletiers were one of two founding families of Saint-Roch-des-Aulnaies. Arriving from Beauport in 1641, Jean Pelletier (1627-1698), son of Guillaume, established himself at Saint-Roch- des-Aulnaies in 1679, with his wife Anne Langlois (1637-1704). They are buried in the cemetery in Rivière-Quelle."*

> *"The land ceded to Jean Pelletier by Nicolas Juchereau in 1679 (the seigneur), in the territory of the Aulnaies, remains to this day property of his direct descendants."*

This was created by L'Association des Familles Pelletier Inc. August 7, 1998. This memorial confirmed that I had visited the correct site at the municipal park a few kilometres back. Other information was available as I inquired further. The unique stone used to support the commemorative plaque comes from the farm "Beau-Prés" of Saint-Roch-des-Aunais, which belongs to Real and Placid Pelletier. It thus comes from the ground having belonged to the ancestor Jean.

The *Seigneurie des Aulnaies* was stated to be the only interpretation site that fully explains the French Seigneurial regime in North America. Unfortunately, the museum building was built over one hundred years after my ancestors left this area. This is the downside of descending, not from one of many pioneering families, but from an original founding family. As I continued east, the next small town was Rivière-Quelle where my journey to the cemetery was similar to other discoveries. As usual, I did not experience an investigative search. The tombstone honouring Jean and Anne Pelletier was just a few feet to the side of the main gate. The rock tomb was large and the writing and family crest was clear.

There are interesting contradictions for many of us who research our family backgrounds. My ancestors were a pioneering and labouring people – they had never been of the aristocracy. Yet the existence of a family crest suggests roots of nobility. This apparent contradiction– a noble crest bestowed upon a family of labourers - is two fold. First, it is clear that the seigniorial system- or the lordly administration, as it maybe called in English – included my family only as habitants. They were not *lords of the manor*. Habitants were farmers who had been granted the use of land by the lord or seignior. In this arrangement, the seigneur is the aristocracy. In medieval Europe the levels of peerage had been numerous, and related to the historic feudal background of the specific land controlled. As a Western Canadian, I found it impossible to relate to this type of value in conditional land use.

The second contradiction is found in that both the logo and the crest were originally granted to Barthelèmyle Pelletier for leading one battle in the fourteenth century that would aid the king. However, never was a king of France a benefactor of the people - a major revolution against this kind of absolutism has obviously transpired since. After his military efforts on behalf of the king, Barthelèmyle Pelletier became a labourer and a merchant. The use of title for privilege for members of his low social rank was virtually non-existent.

However, the opposite maybe true in considering the multitude of descendants who share the very old name of Pelletier. Perhaps because of sheer numbers the family may be legitimate in declaring pride, along with the thousands of other unrelated Pelletiers who share the family crest. In this present era of equality, it is a valid and forward-thinking concept.

* * *

Sandy beaches line the many bays and coves of Kamouraska, the birthplace of two generations of my ancestors, but their origins were often difficult to trace. Because three generations lived here in more recent times, I expected a less abstract trail.

Pierre and Marie-Madeleine Pelletier moved here in 1757, when Kamouraska was a small seigneury. Jean-Baptiste was involved in the former community and had lived here from 1768 to 1827. Célestin and Justine Aubut Pelletier lived here until relocating to New Brunswick in that same year. Gradually Kamouraska stabilized into a quiet agricultural area and a town of seven hundred people.

However when my ancestors left, Kamouraska was a packed Seigneury of 5,500 people. It had been a place of historical significance; now it was a place for tourists such as myself to indulge in their family's past. On a good summer weekend the permanent population often doubled.

As I drove around town, I was not surprised that only two streets serviced most of the traffic. Tourism is the area's largest industry, and the locals' primary source of income. It was promoted as a region of memory, of history and of culture. Every old building had been restored and presented in all its former glory. I found a restaurant where I would return often; this would give me a base. *La Cosette* had a menu du jour that gave me a good sampling of the local food. The waitresses were patient and courteous, putting me at ease with my often tentative, stilted French. To my surprise, I had no trouble understanding their local accent; as for them, they were used to tourists from around the world. Highway No. 132 brought them customers from every corner of the planet, all attempting to speak in a language close enough to French to be comprehensible. As with other languages, its speakers converse with widely varying levels of fluency. If English-speaking tourists wanted to learn French, now was their opportunity.

Also this town seemed to be where the scholarly from Montreal came to spend the less expensive summer vacations, which boded well for the town's future. Art galleries flourished in Kamouraska – its Quebec City and Montreal patrons obviously enjoyed the local art. In proportion to the town, the museum was large. I had now visited a number of museums in Quebec but the period of my primary interest were usually earlier than the museums main focus.

In Kamouraska, I was attempting to find local exhibits from between 1757 and 1827. I was not disappointed. Three floors of the museum were alive with detail from the specific eras of my ancestors. One of the guides in particular was excited at the prospect of discussing museum pieces and exhibits that coincided with my family history. He and I checked out every farm and blacksmith tool. Oxen harnesses, diplomat buggies, one horse sleighs, snowshoes and many other items on display in this museum also belonged to the lives of my ancestors. I had now followed these ancestors through six generations and four family farms. This museum has artifacts and implements from all of them.

In Kamouraska, I stood on the south bank of the St. Lawrence and remembered that a fellow Pelletier had once told me, "You're from the south bank Pelletier family". Now it made sense.

I stood and enjoyed the grandiose panorama of the St. Lawrence from the foot of the town. I had not been able to visit the Pelletier farm here, but perhaps even that was symbolic. We had moved on. Sometimes through history, we can see what we were. Sometimes we see what we didn't have and understand ourselves better.

From my vantage point, on the south bank, there existed alternately both the densest of fogs and the most beautiful of sunsets. I was completely immersed in its tradition. But Célistin Pelletier had moved on and now so would I.

Rivière du Loup was to be my turning off point from Highway 132. From here I would leave this phase of my family history and follow their quest for survival to what is now New Brunswick. However, I would find that two things are relevant to the town of Rivière du Loup.

First I became lost. I had pulled in for gas at one of the ubiquitous Pelletier Motors stations – the Pelletiers were very much alive and well on the south bank of the St. Lawrence – and in doing so, I missed a road sign to the new highway. Simply heading east by accident led me to an interesting new adventure. I had inadvertently taken a route that wound through small villages whose names were oddly familiar – they were names I had heard in newscasts or in stories passed down from other Pelletiers.

Next, I found a connection with Rivière du Loup that harked back to my young adulthood in Vancouver of the 1970s. My first wife had two good friends – sisters – who also became close friends of mine, along with one of their brothers. In discussion with them later, I learned that, in my wrong turn, I had unknowingly driven past the very farm where they had grown up. I was astonished to discover that my friends had lived only twenty kilometres from where generations of Pelletiers had lived. Canada is in many ways, an enormous country, very much linked in the smallest, most integrate ways. We are a country of very alike people and this fact now seemed more relevant to me than ever before.

# Chapter 13 - Timely Reflections

I had been moving steadily east up the south bank of the St. Lawrence River and now continued my *family site drive* to St. Basile inthe same direction. It was only a short drive onto the county of Madawaska, New Brunswick, through hills dotted with gorgeous small villages in picturesque valleys, each unique and yet tinged with an ineffable sameness. In these towns, time had stood still for the last few decades and I reminded myself that for this reason, the town's youth were always leaving for more exciting opportunities in the cities, only to return if their agricultural roots beckoned them. Just before the provincial border I again connected with the Trans-Canada Highway and the consistency of the ever-present MacDonalds and Tim Hortons.

I was by now in the habit of stopping at the first provincial information building for maps after crossing each border. There was one in every Canadian province situated within a kilometre or two of each border on this great highway and they seemed more substantial like international borders in size. Apart from the break in driving, I found – being frugal – free maps, and more important, friendly, helpful information. Oftentimes I might easily have overlooked some of the local sights, either by not realizing that they were close to my planned route, or that they even existed. New Brunswick was no exception.

Upon entering I quickly made use of the free Internet service to email my son and daughter. I wanted to let them know exactly where I was along my journey on our family's historical path. Having picked up a few select brochures from the racks,

I approached one of the amiable staff, outlining my route, and my plan of a few weeks - posed as a question. We began with my first planned stop. I was within an hour of Edmundston and, to my surprise, less than a two-hours drive to St. François. My new *guide* explained that Clair had two motels whereas St. François had only one. Neither was a large town; confirming to me that my visit would be very laid-back. I merely wanted to hangout in the birthplace of my father and grandfather.

As a guide, she continued, "You will definitely want to visit the Daigle home in Clair." "Yes," I replied, "I definitely will."

"It's now right in the town. They've built a small farm with old buildings brought in from close by. They have them in a fenced area that resembles an authentic town. It's right in Clair."

"Was the Daigle home on a farm, just outside of Clair toward Baker Brook?" I asked, finding the conversation to be amazing. I had only just arrived and I was already talking to a complete stranger – and we were being somewhat personal about my family history.

"Yes, and it was built in 1848 by Augustin Daigle."

"Yes, I know. I have a photograph of it. My two aunts visited it when it was on the farm, a couple of decades ago." I finally realized that the conversation was simply coincidental.

She went on to say that it would be worth a visit as it had just been refurbished and restored to its original condition of the mid-nineteenth century. She showed me photographs of the home in both provincial and county tourist brochures.

I felt very much at home. As if just to prolong the exquisite moment, I replied slowly, "I know the home, my grandmother Edith Daigle grew up in it."

She smiled with enthusiasm, and reached for more brochures. We examined other sites in New Brunswick and I organized a circle tour of the province. I returned to the road laden with maps and brochures, and drove on to one of the motels in Clair. I felt very much like I was returning home. All that would be missing were freshly baked cookies on my grandmother's kitchen table.

I had grown up as the only Pelletier in a number of small towns in Alberta and British Columbia. When my mother had remarried she changed her last name, but I had kept mine. I was now touring in an area where not only was my surname commonplace, but even the name of my grandmother was flaunted. I couldn't help smiling a good deal. Western Canada has a prejudice against French-Canadians simmering just below its surface; it seems almost to be an ingrained tradition. I had grown up with this and become complacent about it, but I had not forgotten my roots, my history and my lineage. Now it was all being substantiated.

The visit the next day through the actual home in Clair was not of itself, emotionally significant. In order to create the 1848 environment, the furnishings and artifacts had logically come by donation from a variety of sources, since the Daigle family would have upgraded their own furnishings to a newer style. The house itself had formerly been located on a farm that was purchased for its land and its agricultural value. The new farmer had donated the house, rather than demolish it.

On the prairies thousands of such abandoned homestead houses have been torn down, as farms are expanded and the old buildings rendered useless – unless they were used temporarily for grain storage. The real significance to me lay in the fact that the home was a part of the museum community. It was demonstrated that the history I was pursuing was also important to others, and that seemed to validate my journey.

My grandmother's ancestors had initially built two churches. Joseph Daigle built the first in 1786 and a second in 1790. His grandson Jean-Baptiste Daigle built the third church in1818. The church of this museum farm was a replica of the last two combined, and as such it was new construction.

Finding the first location of the Daigle farm of my grandmother's ancestors almost involved actual investigative research. I can say *almost* in jest. So far in my journey, finding everything had been overly simple. No signs were posted on the highway for Daigle Island so I decided to read my family notes - for years they had existed in a shoebox and I would now finally use them. A forty-year old note, handed down to me from my Aunt Eva, stated it was "off the Baker Brook area."

A local book now out of print, *Histoire du Madawaska*, made it clear that the second farm was "on the north shore, north arm across from Daigle Island." Following the directions was easy; there was only one island with farms on it, directly south of the outskirts of Baker Brook, on the St. Johns River. After taking photographs of the island, I paused for reflection and then carried on.

Later at an information booth in the larger town of Edmunston, I was able to confirm with a lady from the area that I had actually found the island pioneered by Joseph Daigle in 1779. Joseph's son, Jean-Baptiste and Marie Trahan Daigle owned the second farm. Their son was Augustin Daigle, followed by Zepherin Daigle. Finally I experienced *where* they had lived along with *when*.

Simon Daigle had arrived in Acadia and married Madeleine Gautrau at Grand'Pre prior to the year of the expulsion of 1755. It was his son, Joseph Daigle, who had moved to Madawaska and Daigle Island. For me descending from *Acadian* stock was never as well defined as on this day. I later returned for a second and more prolonged observation.

I then drove on to St. François. Over the next few days I would drive on every road crisscrossing the entire community once or twice. However, it was the initial drive into the town itself that seemed perfect. I was entering the birthplace in 1866 of my grandfather and constantly seeking clues, signs, and evidence, from one hundred years ago that might reflect his youthful existence. It was a very picturesque village with the typical dominant church steeple on the single main street. But my specific lineage had left there in 1901, so I only half-expected to find any remnants of our family past.

Immediately I booked into the only motel in town – *Le Relais* - for a couple of days. Maintained in a pristine like new condition, as was my observation throughout both Quebec and New Brunswick. The buildings are much older in general than in the west, however *the east* takes pride in well-kept manicured lawns, trimmed shrubs and hedges, freshly painted fences and siding, and an overall spotless appearance to the homes. In Rural Western Canada we seem to rely on nature to provide natural ambiance.

As I checked in, the lady behind the desk noted my surname with interest, and I mentioned that, " my father and grandfather were born here". She promptly suggested I "drive out to the Pelletier Lumber site, just outside of town." I smiled and explained that even though my ancestors had a lumber mill here, this would not necessarily be the same one. It seemed too easy– to be informed of my great-grandfather's lumber mill site just five minutes after arriving in town. I still wanted to experience *real investigative searching*. Nevertheless, I knew that I would visit there, however skeptical I remained at the moment.

I spent the balance of the day touring about the town, and finally at day's end, located the small one-room village library. I was on its steps as it opened the following morning. My visit there included a meeting with two librarians who made me feel at home with my French and they also found an extra book in their stock to sell to me. It was specifically *The History of Saint-François- de-Madawaska 1859 to 1984*.

In it were six pages referencing the work of my great-uncle Joe. He was the one brother of my grandfather who had not moved west. He had disagreed with my grandfather; and he was determined that there still could be a future for him in Madawaska. In frustration, his four brothers said their goodbyes and left the area that they truly loved. Uncle Joe then became a Member of the Legislative Assembly for the area, and later was appointed high sheriff.

One of the librarians gave me the name and phone number of a Pelletier in Edmundston whom I knew would be a distant relative. She quickly phoned to see if he was home but there was no answer. The younger librarian asked me if I had been out to the Pelletier Lumber Mill site yet. With this kind of repetition, I knew that this site must be relevant.

My next stop was the only museum in St. François. It was a former blacksmith shop. In taking a tour, I mentioned, the general purpose of my visit. The young guide asked: "Have you been out to the Pelletier Lumber site yet?"

"How do you know about the Pelletier Lumber site? " I asked. "It seems to be that most people know where it is."

"We learn about it in school," she said matter-of-factly. "It was the first industry here." This young lady went on to explain that she was a Pelletier on her mother's side; however, she wasn't related to me, as "it was a different Pelletier".

I finally drove out to the mill site. It was easy to find, as they had all told me to turn right onto *Pelletier Road* and to drive to the end. I photographed both the signage and what appeared to be the site, but I could only guess at the exact location. Near a winding creek, in a pastoral open meadow, burned out spots provided evidence of where buildings once stood. The soil was so compacted that nothing could grow on the large rectangular spots. Still unsure as to whether I was viewing the exact location, and therefore feeling somewhat emotionally detached, I photographed the site and left.

I had calculated that one of my last stops in St. François would be the new general store. My uncle Joe had owned one here from 1904 to 1912; I wanted to find out if the present-day *Shop-Easy* store had possibly evolved from my uncle's. When I approached the manager with my question, he suggested we query the hardware manager, who was married to a Pelletier. After a brief conversation, we confirmed that this had not, in fact, been a Pelletier store, and that his wife was from another Pelletier line.

Then the hardware manager proceeded to ask me – I was getting used to this by now – whether I had been out to the Pelletier Lumber site yet.

"Yes, briefly," I replied, "But I didn't know if it was the actual site."

With authority, stating that he had lived here all of his life, he said, "It's exactly where the patches in the field are, directly beside the creek. I'm one hundred percent sure that's where the machinery and buildings were. My grandfather worked there."

The store manager went on to ask how he knew the location, so many years later, and so well.

"My mother also went to school at the Pelletier's Mill School", stated the hardware manager.

"Really– so of course you would know it."

"No, actually," the other man hesitated, "It's where we all used to park when we were teenagers. We didn't have a *drive-in movie theatre* here, so we parked at the Pelletier's Mill site with our girlfriends and messed around there – as much as we dared – probably two or three generations of us!"

The two men looked at each other and chuckled, recalling a shared past of youthful escapades. We all shared knowing that they had somehow created a humorous situation of the well known *parking spot* of Pelletier's Mill – with the dead end road and the unique creek, secluded by trees set in a clearing.

With fresh emotions, I returned to the site. As I slowly walked across it again, contemplating the stream, the terrain and the sky, I began to feel a true kinship with the ancestors who had toiled to establish themselves here. Rémi Pelletier had built and had opened this mill in 1880 with ten employees. I could imagine one of those employees now, for I had by chance met one of his descendants.

\* \* \*

My visit to the cemetery of St. François would produce answers to questions I hadn't even thought to ask. Great-Uncle Joe had a family of nine children, and other Pelletier families had come and gone. However, one of the older graves gave me considerable pause. It was that of my great uncle Fred's very young second wife. He died when I was a preschooler, and I had only heard the legends of his misanthropy and stubborn refusal to speak English.

The gravestone read, as translated from French, *"To The Memory of Amanda Cyre, spouse of Fred Pelletier, who died August 1, 1917."* To its right was a second gravestone. It referred to the son of Fred Pelletier. The epitaph read: *"Johnny Pelletier, spouse of Chantal Michard, died on November 3, 1918, at age 24, 7 months and 26 days."* I could only conclude that in December of 1918, following a loss of his immediate family, Fred Pelletier had joined his brothers in Coleman, Alberta, and he later followed the family to my birthplace, in Dawson Creek, British Columbia. He was a broken man for a reason. I now understand this answer to a question I hadn't ever asked.

\* \* \*

In Edmundston, I had only one mission, something I'd wanted to do all my life. It was a small thing, meaningless to anyone else, but very personal to me. For as long as I could remember, I had possessed a photograph of my father in his teens, posed on a park bench with a group of friends or family with a bridge as the backdrop. I located the bridge and from memory established the angle from which the photo was taken. It was no longer a park, but an industrial area, so I took a few shots to be verified upon my return home. I felt a sense of satisfaction that day: at sixty-one years of age, I'd finally traced the origin of a photo I'd held dear all my life. The background clearly shows the bridge, which I was now able to verify as being built the year before the photo, at the Canada-U.S. border crossing. The date coincided with Emile Pelletier's visit in the year he had been discharged from the Canadian army. With a smile of achievement, I drove onto the newly landscaped Edmundston Park to take part in the city's annual *"Foire Brayonne"*.

In passing a war monument I noticed two local *Pelletier boys* had served to their death. Leon Hubert Pelletier died in WWII of 1939 - 1945 and Albert Pelletier died in the Korean War of 1950 -1953. Even though these men were not closely related, I was reminded of Western Canadian prejudice at the perceived lack of French-Canadian involvement in wars, and I paused respectfully on their behalf.

At the university, The Museum of Madawaska, provided me with two more books. The provincial review of the forest industry included *Pelletier's Mill* and confirmed its start-up date of 1880 by Rémi. The bicentennial booklet for St. Basile included photographs from the old town.

St. Basile was now a part of the city of Edmondston, I lingered there for one week. It was here that Célestin Pelletier settled in1827. My quest for the experience of a *detailed and difficult investigative search* was again met with failure: the farm was well marked with signage. I walked the three city-blocks area shown by *rue Pelletier St*. (All signs in New Brunswick are bilingual). As I took my photographs my heart was warmed by thoughts of my ancestral past. It seemed very honourable to have grown potatoes, grains and flax for clothing here. I tented for the week, three blocks away, at *Camping Ground Iroquois*, 1318 Rue Principale, St.-Basile, New Brunswick.

Rémi Pelletier was born here; the site is now suburbs and real estate development. He and his wife had given up on farming to try a different, and more academic lifestyle. It was Rémi who in 1880 had moved to St. François, taught school, became a notary public, and had opened the lumber mill - with his wife, Philomene Martin Pelletier. I have a photograph of her. She is in informal dress, with her hair made up high in the regal fashion of the day. She seems very stately and dignified, with the kind of soft beauty in the 1880s manner that only the ladies of that era possessed.

\* \* \*

The fact that I was not just visiting the homes of ancestors but also of my father was about to hit me profoundly. As a child, I spent very little time with my father. He died when I was just turning twelve and we had not lived together since I was six. For that reason, he seems to more like an ancestor to me. Now I was about to visit his school. Visiting their father's school is a pilgrimage that many people make. I'm sure everyone finds it an emotional event to some degree. To me it was a catharsis.

The school was a convent called Hôtel-Dieude Saint-Joseph, built in eighteenth-century formal tradition. My aunts and uncles all attended school here. When my grandmother had died with the birth of my father's youngest sibling, this is where he was sent to live and be schooled through to high school completion. It was an orphanage as well as a Catholic residential School. Founded in 1873, for many years it did not change in scope or philosophy. I entered the massive double front doors with no knowledge of what I was seeking. Somehow, appropriately, a museum of its past years is maintained on the site. An elderly nun obliged by showing me around the entire premises including the museum. Upon her husband's death in the Second World War she joined the order, and in the ensuing years had collected an abundance of detailed information.

Unfortunately, all of the school records from the years before were lost in two fires that had burned part of each of the administrative buildings. Happily, my aunts and uncles had referred to the Convent often enough– I did not need written confirmation.

We toured the buildings where my father had walked, played and studied, and I sat in the chapel in exactly his pew. As I walked in the footsteps of his youth, the man that I had never really known was more alive now than ever before. My tour guide seemed to understand well.

As my tour progressed, I found myself hoping that the school had not felt like a prison to my prior generation, as it now seemed to me. I always knew that it was a lifestyle quite different than that which they went on to live in Western Canada. It was monastery in feeling, and eighteenth century coldness in architectural look.

I left with a history book of the convent that covers the years from 1873 to 1973. My father may be in one of the school's group photos from the applicable dates. However, the groups were huge, such that each student's face became only a tiny blurred image. His teachers, however, were individually photographed and listed in the book.

I left *Hôtel-Dieu de Saint-Joseph de Saint-Basile* knowing that I had just gotten to know my father much better. The experience of this single morning was worth the drive of six thousand kilometres across Canada.

My last evening in the county of Madawaska was spent at the provincial park near Saint-Jacques almost abutting Edmundston. I took in the theatrical performance of *L'Acadie des Terres et Forêt en Fête,* which will remain influential to me. Not only was I was very moved by this presentation of an ancestry I shared, but I enjoyed immensely the fact that a number of the young singers and actors shared my family names of both Pelletier and Daigle. It presented a contradiction of Acadian life that would require future study and contemplation on my part. But I decided to put such thoughts on hold until my journey ended. Reconciling the reality of the Acadian expulsion years; is a complex, often philosophical matter.

Throughout my life, my aunts have impressed upon me the fact that I am of Acadian ancestry– half of my *French-Canadian being*. However, my family had chosen to leave Acadia for a better future, and many other Acadians are scattered around the world having been motivated in a similar way. But what was easy to declare even fifty years ago by my aunts and uncles does not hold true today. Only a few weeks earlier, I hadn't felt particularly French- Canadian. Now I was attempting to ascertain whether I was truly harbouring *being d'Acadie*. I will always be emotionally moved however, by the memory of the thought provoking presentation of *"L'Acadie des Terres et Forêt en Fête,"* with which I identified.

\* \* \*

Fredericton, New Brunswick is not a tourist destination, although I'm sure that the people of this good provincial capital would perhaps disagree. I went there for two reasons: Joseph Daigle had visited there in petitioning for land for the Acadians in 1770; as well my great-uncle Joe Pelletier had worked there as an MLA. With this in mind a tour of the Parliament building was my first endeavour. After the tour was complete, I enquired whether there was any further information, available with respect to great-uncles era.

I was excited when the guide offered me what was in effect, a second tour. She showed me the parliament chambers and lounge, where photographs of each legislative setting hung. The stiff, formal poses of each man in the photos put me in mind of an elite gentlemen's club, exclusive of women, who were in any case not allowed to vote prior to 1919. Among these distinguished gentlemen, there was my great-uncle Joe, fulfilling my purpose for visiting these chambers. I took photographs, enjoying the moment. All my life I had heard about his work here, and now the fact was validated.

Next, the young guide took me to the parliamentary library for an introduction to the head librarian. Through quick data based research, they were able to provide me with copies of information from their books on great-uncle Joe. The librarian informed me that the library service was for MLAs and, as a family member I was part of the system. I was made to feel very welcome here in New Brunswick– at home, one might even say.

I was now ready and eager to travel onto Saint John, the city of my father's birth. Paul-Emile Pelletier was born there January 28, 1899; he died on the opposite coast in 1954 at fifty-six years of age. At the time of his birth, his family lived in St. Francois but my grandmother was taken to the larger hospital in St. John for the birth.

Today, this is a city that is worthy of being a tourist destination. I enjoyed the New Brunswick Museum, observing the Bay of Fundy tides and marveling over the fact that this was Vancouver's, opposite shore. My visit to the *Museum's*

*Archives and Research Library* produced more results – and it appeared I was finally about to experience my long awaited *investigative research.* Well almost - everything that I wanted to know was already available in published books. It was exciting to see the originals of both manuscripts and historical documents, many of which related directly to my family. Every province has such a library, but this one will remain special.

I happened to park in front of the Saint John county courthouse, a building that was constructed of stone before 1900. Upon recognizing a research possibility, I immediately took the public building tour. I was now curious about what a *high sheriff* was - a newly discovered title of great-uncle Joe's that I wanted to decipher. If the information existed anywhere, this would surely be the place.

When I queried the staff, and as a particular surprise, I was able to meet immediately and privately with the sheriff of the county. She and I shared the humor that as not being one, when she had taken over her office, she also had not known what the title meant either. She had gone through a process of research and discovered that it was an official appointment, as opposed to a government posted application process.

In Uncle Joe's case, it was an appointment directly by the King of England. It was a duty to participate in ceremonies, when the Lieutenant Governor of the province was not available. Needless to say the job encompassed other duties such as heading the sheriff's department.

In reflecting on the more recent history of New Brunswick, the political need to have French- Canadian individuals in higher provincial office provided a legitimate reason for this type of appointment. Uncle Joe was one of two men whose professional profiles had become well known throughout the province, particularly with regard to their insistence on French language being used within the provincial parliament.

Concurrently, French-speaking representation needed to be shown to the provincial population. Joe Pelletier was the right man for the job of heading the sheriff's department as this would be well documented. The appointment had come from the King in London England, and in that there was political strategy. Uncle Joe died very young, with cardiac problems that had been related to high stress. Such were his personal choices and challenges.

New Brunswick is a province that presents its past to all tourists with great panache. Unfortunately, I may have missed observing its present era, as I spent most of my time there living within the dimensions of another century. I will leave the enjoyment of present-day New Brunswick for another trip.

# Chapter 14 - Naught But Tradition Remains

The next destinations on my tour were Prince Edward Island and Nova Scotia, returning on the east coast of New Brunswick. There I would find the two Acadian sites that had been known to me most of my life. The first was Grand Pré, Nova Scotia, and the second was the Historic Acadian Village at Caraquet in New Brunswick, which had now evolved and grown into the big leagues as a tourist attraction.

At first observation, the Grand Pré site seemed more a depiction of Longfellow's romantic poem *Evangeline* than it was a reference to Acadia as a real place with real people. As I toured the site, I knew better than to attempt to put that difference into words, since so many writings have already tackled that particular task exceedingly well. As a poem written by someone who had never been in the area then known as Acadia, and who had not actually partaken in the culture, it had achieved the not inconsiderable feat of announcing to the world exactly what, who, and where Acadia was. Aside from establishing the myth of Evangeline, the poem almost single-handedly established Acadia's identity.

Having read *Postcards from Acadie* by Barbara Le Blanc, and agreeing with her, it seems there's little left for me to say. The descendants of the Acadian deportation over the years from 1755 to 1763 have been well-regarded and shown great respect in Grand Pré. Prior to reading *Postcards from Acadie*, I felt somewhat guilty at my conclusion that the relationship to the tourism industry was an integral part of Grand Pré. Knowing that this is a deliberately orchestrated image, fostered by all pure Acadians involved, has now set my mind at ease.

The most relevant issue is that my grandparents had not been particularly concerned with the deportation itself. My grandmother, Edith Daigle was a pure Acadian by definition. Stanley Pelletier, my grandfather was the first non-Acadian spouse within the Daigle family line. However, neither family were involved in the expulsion. War had existed in the Grand Pré area for almost one hundred years. Many Acadians had been asked to leave their land and many like the Daigles, simply did. To these Acadians, the expulsion represented a so-called changing of the guard. Throughout the history of the world, the fact that governments have not been kind to the toilers of the land has been a reality of human existence, and it was no different for those having to leave the area and start again. That is not to make light of that fact, but to deal with it as a reality.

As such, the deportation as depicted in Longfellow's Evangeline, is not the history of all Acadians. The Expulsion of Acadians is an all-encompassing issue over a number of years. The elements of weather, the erratic behaviour of some of the native groups, the difficulty in obtaining sufficient supplies – all these things presented their initial hardships. Having to be uprooted at the whim of government was on this list of challenges.

These were very hardy people; they were strong in ways unfamiliar to most twenty-first century individuals. After a lot of contemplation, I would finally leave Grand Pré, not harbouring the myth of Evangeline, but marveling at the strength of the Acadians continual hard labour, and most of all of their determination to survive and succeed with their families in this new land.

\* \* \*

At this point, two ideas struck me. First, I acknowledged that Simon Daigle and Madeleine Gautrea had met and married here in Grand Pré. I had already visited the Daigle home of my grandmother in Clair, New Brunswick and it was obvious that as both a cultural and an economic group, they had succeeded in all of their efforts. Any sympathy or even empathy, bestowed by the public in general, was not wanted nor needed. My Acadian ancestor, had focused on understanding the expulsion problem, had formulated a plan for their work in Madawaska, and had worked their plan to its final success. They had rebuilt their community.

The second concept that suddenly became clear was the fact that only my grandmother was Acadian. I needed the understanding of there being two branches of that larger and general French-Canadian family. Throughout my life, my aunts in Western Canada had pointed out that I was Acadian. They had a vested interest in this; their mother had been Acadian and much less prejudice existed against those who were known as Acadians than against those thought of as French-Canadian. There is little logic in this, but it was the Western Canadian philosophy of the time.

As simple as it sounds, this was the bottomline for me – my grandmother's ancestors were Acadian. My grandmother was Acadian. My family was French-Canadian. My father was French-Canadian and spoke French as a first language. My two offspring both speak French as a second language. My daughter graduated from high school with French exams - it was a first language in Program Cadre, a curriculum that was seventy percent French. Even in British Columbia it was quite different from the French Immersion Program, which is only thirty percent French content. The site at Grand Pré was meant to reveal and inspire the process of identity reconstruction. As I visited and learned more about my roots, it was helping me achieve the same goal. It was finally formulated – *my grandmother was Acadian– I am French-Canadian*. At least that's close. I could now travel on to the next Acadian sites feeling somewhat organized and clear about nationality issues.

I had now read at length and visited the museums thoroughly enough to realize that Acadia's ambiguity in terms of both history and geography, exists throughout both the Maritimes and Quebec. The only fact on which everyone agrees is that Acadians are descendants of the people deported in the eighteenth century. The Expulsion included those who were not comfortable remaining in their hostile communities. In 1755 there were 2,200 people living in the greater Grand Pré area. That translates into a lot of descendents.

Port Royal, now named Annapolis Royal was where the young Jean Daigle and his father, Joseph, and mother Madeleine, lived for a year or so until 1763. They had moved from the Ile St. Croix, where Jean was born. When I visited, the small island of St. Croix was celebrating its four-hundred-year anniversary as a settlement.

I spent a good deal of time visiting the reconstruction of the Habitation (fort) at the Port Royal National Historic Park. It was billed as being faithful in detail to the original buildings designed by Samuel de Champlain, one of the founders. The layout is accurate and structures formed a compact square around the centre courtyard. It was complete with a palisade and a cannon platform. The buildings included the governor's residence, a chapel, the kitchen, a blacksmith's shop and a fur-trading room.

The most popular room was the dining hall where, in 1606, for the purpose of boosting morale, Champlain formed the colony's first social club. It was called, *The Order of Good Cheer*. Here, each member took his turn as the Grand Master and was responsible for the feast of game and wine. Champlain had described its reason for being, as a motivator of men. Marc Lescarbot, lawyer and playwright, wrote and produced a play here, the same year of its inauguration.

Two hundred and fifty years later, Théophile Hamel created an oil painting of the room and its former occupants based on scant documentation. This Hamel rendering was the basis for the reconstruction of the Habitation in 2004. Considering that log cabins of the day had only six-foot-high ceilings, it seems improbable that the nine-foot ceilings of the present-day reconstruction are an accurate portrayal of the original rooms. Architectural composition in art is a calculation and so were the high ceilings relative to the painted scene. Therefore the new Habitation structures most likely are only faithful to the mid-nineteenth-century painting.

Visitors to these historic replicas of Champlain's original buildings might want to reserve a measure of healthy skepticism of the claim that they are "faithful in every detail to the original buildings as designed by Champlain." It is always wise to question the veracity of presented history.

The site was very interesting and I was intimately familiar with the history; however I did not feel an emotional attachment. Perhaps my extensive reading had left my imagination too set with its own mental images of the period. Or it might have been that the reconstruction had too much of a movie industry look to it. Whatever the reason, the site did not inspire or further the process of personal identity for me. Perhaps I was now trying to deal with the validity of two French speaking groups of people not being the same in race, creed and nationality. Still, I considered this a remote possibility as the two years difference in settlement, and a few hundred kilometers, were unlikely to have created two peoples and two cultures.

After enjoying being a tourist in Nova Scotia, I returned to New Brunswick and this time enjoyed the drive up the Eastern Coast, which borders the Gulf of St. Lawrence. This highway would join my return route and I was driving on the so-called Acadian Coast visiting sites throughout the Acadian Peninsula. For someone from the Pacific Coast – who had been told that Acadia was a distinct place and time in history–this process was thought provoking. I was on my way to the *Historic Acadian Village* at Caraquet and still looking for uniqueness.

At the village, I found specific Acadian ancestry and its relevance to my personal journey. Presented here were merchants, innkeepers, woodworkers, a blacksmith, a tinsmith, a shingle maker, a broom maker, and farmers - each with an authentic costume from the past. Visits ensued to a printing shop, a mill, a school, a chapel, a lobster hatchery and a cooperage, all with individuals demonstrating various aspects of life as it had been in seventeenth and eighteenth century Acadia.

I found that my favourite of the small farms at the site was the Cyr Farm. I had never seen oxen, nor had I ever really known how a spinning wheel worked.

As if to underline my perceptions of Acadia and French-Canadian life being one - in the smallest shed, flax was being beaten. A few feet away in the house, they showed me how they worked with the newly prepared flax. Next they gave a demonstration of spinning it. They were making cloth out of flax. I was amazed at the process. Millions of people may have had that knowledge and perhaps enjoyed a presentation such as this. I didn't and I hadn't.

In their barn were two longhorned cows. They stood passively in half door stalls facing outward so that we, the tourists, could see their faces. I like cows - *it's in my genes*, so I did what I had done all of my life. I reached out and petted one between its horns. All my life cows have allowed me that one stroke of petting, then they shook and tossed their heads away to prevent a further touch. To my great amazement this cow did something that was similar to my own inclination. It put its head up toward my hand as if seeking more attention. Dogs do that instinctively and sometimes, even cats do it, but cows don't respond like that. I petted it some more. Seeing that the animal was friendly with me, a family drew nearer and the children held out straw scraped from the floor for its feed. The animal's partner joined it and the two beasts with long horns munched away while the children petted them. The obvious finally occurred to me. They weren't cows - they were oxen.

I was a man of world travel and I had lived on a home-stead with my maternal grandparents; we even had range cows. I had simply forgotten my elementary school lessons on early Canada. Oxen were used and they were domestic. After I had petted the oxen a few more times, still in amazement, I returned to the shed to ask the obvious question. "Were oxen always this tame?"

The reply was to someone else, not me (while being the supposed horseman from the west). "Yes", replied the farmer in costume, "they're more domestic than cattle. They were more like family pets."

"Of course", I replied in French as knowingly as possible.

Some people will visit elephants or zebras. I really enjoyed being around those oxen. As I was evaluating my roots, my culture and my ancestry, I became convinced that my affinity with these animals was inherited and in my genes. That fact may not be scientific, but I enjoyed the humor in it.

The Cyr home was a square log house, typical of the Madawaska area. It was handmade using fieldstones and it featured a stove of cast iron parts within a stone masonry. The lady of the house, who in this case was a fine actress, was making a stew. She warmly described her recipe to the surrounding onlookers. I recognized her speech patterns – she had an accent identical tp those of the aunts I had known so well, so many miles away.

Then I reminded myself that my great-uncle Fred Pelletier had married the Cyr girl from just down the road – many years prior. Her former home - this house - had been transported from St. Basile where my great-aunt grew up. The Cyr home had been hauled here to the Historic Acadian Village at Caraquet; piece by numbered piece. As a home built in the early 1800s, it represented the details of family life of this village so well. I wasn't directly related to the Cyr family, however my great-uncle was related by marriage. His father-in-law had built this cabin.

There was a logical, personal, reason that I had never identified with Loyalist History and old English settlements that I had driven past on my journey. Simply I felt I was French-Canadian. I relaxed and enjoyed the rest of the presentations and music taken from the three centuries of rural Acadia.

This was also a day of tasting the food of my ancestors, prepared in the old manner. The Acadian food specialty handed down from the life and times of Joseph Daigle was offered at a replication of a roadside inn. I opted for pot-en-pot - chicken stew cooked with homemade noodles - and poutines rapees, which were made up of large balls of grated and mashed potatoes embedded with diced salt pork simmered in water. Another main dishes offered combined turnips, cabbages or red beans with bacon. As I enjoyed the experience, the taste was a reminder that a lot salt and pepper was available, while many other spices were not. I enjoyed every bite and wished that I too could have dressed for the time and the occasion. Later I returned to the same café to have the poutines rapees with molasses as a dessert.

The Historic Acadian Village wasn't about the expulsion. It was about pioneering; it was about hard labour and inventive use of the agricultural methods of the time. This village was about community in a very positive sense. Again I felt that familiar *at home feeling* - I fit in. Interestingly enough, I spoke French throughout the day with a confidence I had never had before experienced. I felt it was my language and if I was making mistakes, so be it. I was in the land of my forefathers and reveling in it. As the day came to a close, I felt that my historic sensitivity had been somehow altered.

Since my journey to Quebec and the Maritimes, I have spent time in France analyzing the emotions it aroused surrounding my Acadian roots. First, I discovered and acknowledged exactly what it meant to be of the five-century Percheron family line, a descendant of those early labourers from the former province of Perche, France. Also, I could now define what it meant to be Acadian.

Those unclear about that definition, tend to make more of Acadian-ness than is necessary. Being Acadian is simply: pride of ancestry, pride of independence, pride of community and pride of hard work on land one could call one's own. The early Acadian families had survived because they held all these traits dear. My grandmother's Acadian family defined their values with four hundred years of Acadian history, yet this did not negate the earlier history from France. To me, finally, the long lineage from Perche to Acadia had come together in a logical, natural way; my life long conflict had been resolved. Extrapolating from this resolution, being at once Western Canadian and French-Canadian did not seem such a great stretch either. My ancestors had entered and left each epoch and each region with some of these identities. Each was separate and each could be celebrated as such; family bonds are strengthened from such celebrations. Weakness in striving for personal goals, on the other hand, comes from negative attitudes and emotions. I was now able to see that none of these identities needed to be seen as negative. In his fresh analysis, even the expulsion of Acadians could be viewed in a positive light.

Seven hours by car and three hundred years separates Beauport, Quebec, from St. François, New Brunswick. During my return trip I retraced much of my original route, stopping a second time at many of my family sites. I reflected that all of my adult life I had procrastinated learning about my heritage in this first hand-way. Perhaps, after all, all that's needed is an outline of a family chronology and a road map. I hope others will follow the same steps I took.

My route was not yet complete, because in somewhat of the same fashion as my grandfather and father, I crossed the Prairies and returned to the West. I knew I was near home when the mountains became silhouettes against the sky. I couldn't help thinking about the terrain of the Canadian Shield being dominantly rock. However as I approached the Rockies looming in the distant horizon, I looked through my front car window and I thought with absurd humour and intent of civic pride: "now that really is rock".

My first visit after crossing the vast and flat prairie was to the Pincher Creek, Alberta museum. Set near the foothills, my great-uncle Henry Pelletier had farmed here. His family grew up here, before they moved to various cities. Pioneer Village Museum was highlighted by a small room with World War I artifacts and memorabilia, some of which related specifically to my father's Calgary battalion. His was the group of young men from this area. It was emotionally moving to be in this place, surrounded by photographs and mementos of my father's comrades. When I began to leave, I checked myself and paused and remembered to slowly walk through one extra time. That is what museums are really for.

Nearby Pelletier Lumber was at a site between Blairmore and Coleman. As I had done in the East, I strolled into the centre of the site, pausing and reflecting on the landscape just as my forefathers had. I gazed upon the serene beauty of Crowsnest Mountain, a view that they also admired. The lumber mill supplied the timbers for the underground mines as well as for the homes and businesses of the hundreds of people rapidly populating the new settlements.

The area is rich with anecdotes of early twentieth century history; I had heard many of them from my aunts and uncles. The Crowsnest Pass Museum represented them again, and I was able to relive the tales. The land was raw, and mine disasters were common. Chaos was more common than peace in these early years, along with the escapades of individuals who were not inclined to respect the little law and order that did exist.

Before travelling on, my day was spent at the Frank Slide Interpretive Centre. I allowed myself the luxury of considering my family to be a part of it, even though they hadn't been.

It was finally time to bid my farewells to this area that had given my family its start in the West, just as many of them bade farewell to it following World War I. When the Pelletier boys returned home from the Great War, they would follow my grandfather to his choice of location in Northern British Columbia – a province thousands of miles from early Acadia and that is now my home base.

The representation of the past is never neutral or objective; time, circumstances and cultural beliefs influence it. The interpretation of history is fluid and it changes in relation to the present. Contemporary perceptions of gender, social status and ethnicity have always played a great role in determining how we view past events and therefore history

I am aware that my own perceptions of my ancestors' odyssey to the Canadian West are also biased, greatly influenced by my upbringing there. But with my long journey and deep investigation, I had now achieved a small milestone: a more balanced, more complete overview of my personal history.

# Chapter 15 - En France

It really began forty thousand years ago with Cro-Magnon man. Subsequently, life in France evolved to a second spécimen, *L'homme de Villeneuve-la-Guyard*, but that is another story. These hardy people were the first primitive farmers in France and they survived their challenges some seven thousand years ago.

My first visit to Paris, France, was in 1965 and it was here that I began my studies in European History and the arts. During the sixties, I lived in Paris for a total of almost three years. Now armed with genealogical information on my Pelletier family lineage, I now returned with a different quest in 2006. I had planned that this journey that would take me outside of Paris, would not be unlike my visit to family sites in Eastern Canada. I began within the city of Paris, knowing that I would visit the former Pelletier farms following.

The documents in the genealogical section of the French National Archives conclude that the Pelletier family from Perche had been descendants of Barthelémy Le Pelletier of Brittany. He had been given much of the Perche forest by Charles Vas a reward for his bravery in the battle of Thouars, in Poitou, August 7, 1372. Exactly when the forests were lost and ceded back to royalty, however, had not yet been established prior to my last visit to France.

Through a bureaucratic process, I was able to become a member and researcher at the National Archives of France, in Paris. It had not been my initial intention to become a researcher, but by  the end of one particular day of inquiries, I had achieved temporary membership. I would have been just as content to be guided by librarians, but this was France and it became clear that if I were to make any headway on my personal historical quest, it would be through my efforts alone. It is now a point of pride that I could humbly enter these hallowed premises, scour through dozens of actual documents of antiquity, and be held responsible for my handling of them.

As a city of museums, Paris hadn't changed much. However, I had never actually been inside the National Archives of France. To now be perusing papers bearing the seals of so many well-known men of history was an exceptional treat. Reading through original documents concerning the colonies, I turned each page carefully and with awe. As if it were contemporary literature, I skimmed through the dispatches and orders given to the colonies from the king, reading from *Textes Sur Le Canada* and *Inventaire Analytique Colonies*. There were continual demands for increased production of goods. In the same document were orders for more production of births. These instructions on human husbandry, written in the cold detached tone of an autocracy that cared for little but money and power, were far removed from the reality and survival of its lower classes (my relatives).

Research is usually conducted through established methodology but often chance plays just as important a role. By sheer luck I came upon the documents that re-established the Perche forests as owned and controlled solely by the king of France. In reading material that at first seemed unrelated, I discovered the specific declaration.

The changes in rights to either seigneuries or to tax collecting had gradually been taken away by an "Arret du Conseil d'Etat". The building of Versailles and the lifestyles of its inhabitants had this effect on all of France. A translation of the declaration reads:

> "A General Receipt of a Forest Pole that had been done in 1619 and 1622, for all the central region of France was given. Letters of Provision accompanied by and an Act of Reception accompanied it. These were submitted during the Audience of France. Having the office to advise the king, and being a general receiver relative to this department, it was declared that all forests were re-conquered in all of any existing forestry matters up to June 18, 1618, and including the accounts of 1619, along with the accounts of 1622."

The "Pole" refers to *forest cruising*, which is the general term in contemporary forestry. The "Audience of France" means a court hearing. All expenditures were also to be reclaimed, that is it was demanded that they be paid back to the king. The document was clear in blanketing the old provinces of "Parys, Isle de France, Brye, Le Perche, and Picardye ePays"

Adjacent to the area of Bresolettes were 3,200 hectares of Perche forest held by a Trappist monastery that had been founded in the twelfth century. My original theory had been that the monks of this monastery, somehow by force or persuasion, had taken away the Pelletier's right to the forest. It seemed logical, for the monks already held much of the surrounding Perche forest and the Pelletier's lived a scant four kilometres away. However, from the archived evidence I discovered, I could now conclude that my theory had been wrong, and that the monks had very little to do with the Pelletiers' loss of the forestry lands. The documents clearly established that the Trappists had negotiated their land contract with the king quite separately.

The many French civil wars from 1562 to 1598 had more to do with it. With these constant changes, being on the winning side, or even the rational side, was almost impossible. In this former era, "The Lord giveth and the Lord taketh away", was a very earthy reality; to such an extent that I really wondered if medieval life was not the root of the expression.

Later, I was able to do further research at the archives of the *Institute National de France* and the *Bibliotheca A Foundatore Mazarinea*, the oldest public library in France. All the material I studied had been in some way affected by the days of the French Revolution. Volumes of irreplaceable works had been destroyed in its chaos. Seemingly unrelated documents can be connected, but only by extensive browsing. There were three related receipts filled; my translations are as follows.

The first was to Fluery Pelletier, who appeared to have been involved in many transactions. *"Gifted to Fluery, manager of the kitchen, for the mouth of the king, a sum of 180 books of tournaments, on the sums of money coming from the sale of trees cut down by a storm in 1519, in the planted area of Neauphlie. Dated at Paris, on September 8, 1518."*

The next receipt stated:

*"Gifted and given to Fluery Pelletier, chef and judge of the kitchen of the king, 12 pounds of tournaments, amounts of lods for the sale of certain acquisitions by him, made to the Feif-of-the-king. Dated June 18, 1537."*

In the last receipt, another Pelletier established the court as a client:

*"Recognized with the treasury of the court savings, to pay Antoine Pelletier, muleteer, 450 pounds of tourois for two large mules of wonder, that the king has purchased from him."*

Unfortunately ancient monetary forms cannot be translated as barter was the established method of purchasing and the terms referred to regional currency.

I found that numerous individuals were also listed under the category of the historic families of Normandie, France. There were twelve families of Pelletiers named.

*1. Pierre Pelletier – the glasswork artist of Lyonnais and Forez.*

*2. The Pelletiers of Paris – made up of many families in France.*

*3. The Pelletiers of Poitou, Auv and Fonds Guillemot.*

*4. The Pelletiers originally from Normandy areas and now in Canada.*

*5. The Pelletiers of Bonnefond d'Oisy and the Pelletier of Doisy.*

*6. The Pelletiers of Chambure, of Las, and of Montbelin.*

*7. The Pelletiers of Clery, d'Escrots or of Crotz.*

*8. The Pelletiers of Gigondas; the parent originally was an army officer.*

*9. The Pelletiers of La Houssaye, originally from Mantes, and established in Paris after the sixteenth century.*

*10. The Pelletiers of Montigny (Poitou)*

*11. The Pelletiers of Montmarie (Beauv.)*

*12. The Pelletiers of Tanqueux (Ile-de-France.)*

I made further discoveries relative to Pelletiers living in France, none of whom were of the same family lineage as Guillaume Pelletier.

*Robert le Pelletier was the Seigneur of Bonne - Mare in 1470. Ecuyer le Pelletier succeeded him.*

*Pierre le Pelletier was born in 1508. He married Jeanne le Royer and became a seigneur.*

*Jeanne Pelletier, a parliamentary lawyer, was assassinated in 1588. He married Madeleine Chauvelin on Feb. 6, in 1583.*

*Louis le Pelletier, Secretary of State of the Department of War in 1624. Michel le Pelletier became the Seigneur of Souzy 1640.*

Most of the area of the Perche Forest is now designated as a natural regional park. My observation as an avid cyclist, is that the extensive public trails found there are some of the finest in the world for bicycling. The lakes are small and pristine, and provide solitude, and great fishing. Five hundred years ago, however, hunting as a sport was the predominant use. The land was private until the time of the French Revolution, when all such lands were finally turned over by a process, to the public government.

I enjoyed a drive through the former estate of the Seigneur D'Alexandre de Lavone. It was now a federal agricultural experimental farm and college, and was lost by their family after three hundred years, in 1755. This land may also now be where it belongs

Within this contemplation of process there is the inferred relationship of the family to royalty, by the root of the name of Pelletier. As a name, it evolved from the trade of being a furrier. The name Pelletier derives from the Latin pellis, which means furrier. It refers to one who buys, sells, or prepares furs or pelts, or more generally one in the fur trade. Bythe fifth century, the taste for rare and valuable fur-lined coats existed. King Charlemagne used to wear a doublet lined with otter skins during the winter. By 1346, the fur merchants of Paris had attained their own special status and privileges. It was not the trapping of animals but the process of importing and marketing the finished product to royalty and the upper classes with which the word Pelletier was connected.

However in French, Pelle means shovel. Pelletée means shovel full. Pelleter means to shovel. Pelleteuse is a construction excavator. Somehow in considering my ancestral Pelletier name and family, this use of language was now more important. Being in construction was more to the point of what I knew to be the contemporary reality of the ancient region. It was also a more probable long-term family condition. "Furrier", however, would be the ongoing acceptable translation.

Now for the first time, I would visit Versailles. I was enough of a purist as a student, when I first lived on the Left Bank of Paris in the mid sixties, that a visit to Versailles was something that I had purposely left to the tourists. At that time, the message of Versailles was the antithesis of everything I believed in. I had never been a hippy; however, I was of a generation that insisted its images, places and icons be relevant. The image of Versailles with its pre-revolution focus; was to me, the ultimate in decadence.

I had retained many images from hours spent in the Louvre during my earlier stay in Paris; in particular, the subjects of Jean-Antoine Watteau's paintings. Watteau was a French rococo painter of the early eighteenth century whose canvasses portrayed the great demarcations of class structure for the period. In essence, they showed the upper classes behaving abominably– at least by today's standards – dropping their soiled handkerchiefs for the lower classes to retrieve – as their lives were depicted without purpose and dilettantish. The women were painted as if they are in a world of fantasy, clothed in rich satins, ample skirts and acting in a bizarre formal manner. Of all the painted subject matter of the pre-revolution century, I despised this the most. Instinctively I knew my ancestors had been members of the subservient class of their time, and I could not view the ostentation and excess of Versailles without thinking of its cost – thousands of human lives in circumstances identical to those of my own family.

The later use of the Chateau of Versailles from where France controlled the ruling classes of Europe by staging an ongoing who's who party– to thus create a political utility by using the flamboyant architecture - was one that I could relate to. It had the positive nature of a study of the ridiculousness of humankind.

By the 1680's Versailles had become the home of the court and the accepted seat of the government. For Louis XIV and numerous other rulers, it was believed that states might best be preserved through expansion. Decisions related to New France were made in this lofty environment, far removed from the reality of pioneering lives, and New France was no more than a dropped handkerchief to this demanding land acquisition strategy.

The veritable explosion of artistic energy from within the arts, as was found at Versailles further removed the royal court from the reality of the lower working people. There emerged a Versailles of marble, a worthy rival of antiquity with an eternal model of deliberate refinement in the arts as its prime focus. The sophistication of music, art, architecture, literature and the performing arts, may have had positive effects for France, but it had a marked deleterious impact to decisions made for the New World. By visiting Versailles, I was standing in the lion's den.

The palace was a frenzy of tourists, but I managed to make my way through them to review it all. This decadent place with the personality of Louis XIV, the Sun King, shining through, was just as the brochures had stated. It was vast and opulent. However, to my surprise, it didn't dazzle me. I had visited many palaces in Europe, all of which billed themselves as second only to Versailles. But herein lies the difference between rococo and the baroque. To many of us, the baroque palaces built one hundred years later were more beautiful.

As a Western Canadian, having grown up among our towering pine trees and majestic Rocky Mountains – I was relieved not to be dazzled. Versailles had been built on the backs of lower-class citizens not unlike the Pelletier family. Those courageous enough sought to escape this tyranny with their departure to the vast unknown– and potential opportunities – of New France.

It was a rainy day when I first viewed the Grand Trianon, lavishly built for the king's mistress, Madame de Maintenon. But this grandiose engineering feat of the time, which so often was revered as being splendid and exotic, was merely a large pond. It was the sculpture and not the water that was significant. I would survive the shock and I was content that I had waited all of these years to visit.

*　*　*

On another day at the Musée d'Orsay, I viewed a painting
that depicted the reality of the Middle Ages. In his 1865, *Scène
de guerre au Moyan Age*, Edgar Degas depicts four nude
woman, as they lie on the ground. They are being trampled to
death by a knight on his horse. Four other women stand in
various helpless positions with a second man on a horse aiming
his arrows at them. The two horses protect the men as one of
them carries loot they have pillaged and the other his choice of
a woman. The painting portrays many of the atrocities of the
sixteenth century and its rigid class structure.

At the Louvre, I was struck by Flemish artist Sébastiaen
Vranck's *Pillage d'un Village* painted in 1589. It was a detailed
depiction of armed warriors battling against unarmed villagers,
with clothing removed from the already dead bodies and
peasants pleading for their lives. Some of the trees are dead,
symbols of both the vanity of the knights and of death itself.
The painting rendered clear class distinctions, similar to the
work of Degas and his similar subject material.

Peter Paul Rubens, in his painting *Un Tournoi,*, showed
two knights fighting two opposing knights. Ornate with
flourishes, his fairy-tale-like composition was consistent with
the ideals of the time – those that esteemed the bravery and
gallantry of knights. Rubens and Vranck were contemporaries.
However, only Vranck can be said to be in touch with the reality
of the late sixteenth century Europe.

By 1600 an *épee de chasse*, a kind of lance had been
developed. It was six feet long, and it was designed for
hunting animals. However, it also had the capacity to stab a
peasant, while the knight remained in a seated position of
safety on his horse. This was not a fair class-war.

It was scenes such as that depicted in Vranck's painting,
not Ruben's that the Pelletier family had left behind in Europe.
To be a farmer in New France was to be a part of a great dream
of a peaceful and productive existence in stark contrast to the
looting and behavior of the class that had created Versailles.

On the positive side, it was in Versailles, at the beautiful Hall of Mirrors in 1919, that the Treaty of Versailles was signed to mark the end of the First World War. That was significant. My father, Emile Pelletier fought in that war. Guillaume had lived just a short distance from Versailles when he made the decision to settle in the New World. I might disrespect Versailles, for the depravity of the era it represented, yet at the same time, it held much historical relevance for me.

As I later toured Paris, I found that the abbots of Cluny had built a Parisian residence in the thirteenth century. In visiting its well-preserved walls and ceilings, and the attached Gallo-Roman baths of antiquity, I could appreciate this museum as it presented the medieval and artistic endeavours. Among the exhibits were a wheat container used in the sixteenth century, along with leather shoes of the same era. I was reminded of visits to museums of my grandfather's era in both Eastern and Western Canada, and I felt humbled that this older museum even existed. Like most visitors, I took photographs in an effort to preserve my awe. This was not about the jewels of kings; it was about a wheat container and some worn leather shoes – even possibly from Bresolettes. I emailed photographs of both to my son. On a prior day, I had almost completely ignored the possibility of viewing the ancient crown jewels at the Louvre.

The Conciergerie was called the palace in the city. In 508 AD, Frankish King Clovis I united Gaul as a kingdom and made Paris his capital, naming it after the original Parisii tribe. About 451 AD, it is said that St. Genevieve victoriously shielded the city from the Huns. Then in the sixth century, Childebert I had a church built there. Hugh Capet established his Royal Council in the palace; however, the most important construction was carried out in the thirteenth century under King Louis IX.

La Conciergerie is a fortress-like building built primarily by King Phillip the Fair in the years 1285 to 1314. One of the finest examples of medieval secular architecture, it has a long history as a place of imprisonment, torture and death. Three round and very typical towers have survived. King John the Good added to the structure in 1350 and a current clock was built in 1585, during Elois Pelletier's early childhood. It is set in a coloured frame, and rather ironically flanked by the allegories of the Law and Justice.

Until the second half of the fourteenth century La Conciergerie had been the residence of King Charles V. It subsequently became a prison that later served the French Revolution. In total 2780 people were sentenced to death and would spend their last moments in the Conciergerie. Of these guillotinés two were members of the Pelletier family who had been left behind in France. F. Pelletier was a *tourneur* – the man responsible for the throwing of mock birds in the air as targets. Jacques Pelletier was a *cafetier*, or coffee maker. Setting up shooting targets, or being a maker of fine coffee were not the problems. However, being a part of the large entourage that served the king cost them their lives.

The records of the guillotiné are now considered accurate and complete. Coincidently in Canada a somewhat naïve process was taking place. In the name of the king, Jean-Baptiste Pelletier was building a church on the south shores of the Saint Lawrence River; he completed it in 1792 and called it Saint-Louis. These individuals of the Pelletier family did not know each other. Yet all of them demonstrated blind devotion to their king, apparently oblivious to the atrocities committed under his reign.

People from around the world visit this site in Paris, many of them intent on one thing only: to view the former cell of Marie-Antoinette. It was my own first visit to a building, which I knew to be of the time of Elio Pelletier. In my mind and spirit, I was visiting the time of my ancestors some five hundred years earlier. When I had lived in Paris so many years ago, I had none of the facts of my family's history in France. Now I was able to conceptualize their lives, and the building helped make it almost tangible.

Among many other such reflections, I would also contemplate the incongruity of the fact that the Louvre was a major castle decorated by Nicolas Poussin by 1643, at the same time the newly arrived Pelletier family was building their first log cabin in the New World. This seemed an enormous dichotomy when related to patriotism of country.

The Château of Fontainebleau was the home of Louis IX, followed by six subsequent kings. This was a Château that predated Versailles by one hundred years. It was both from the time of my ancestors and from their region of France, and I was very excited to be there. In my observing the beauty of the inlaid wood of the most exotic room called *La Galeria* - built for Francois I in 1528, I realized it dated from the very time of Eloi's father. In *La Salle des Gartes*, I first noticed post and beam construction exactly the same as used in Canada by Champlain. Although more elaborate, it was identical to the engineering I had observed in Port Royal, Nova Scotia.

With a little planning, I could stand in each and every room alone – alone with my ancestors. In *La Salle de Bal*, recordings of *Danses de la Renaissance* played. Dragons were portrayed on the walls and I was able to relax and enjoy, as ancestral thoughts flitted through my mind.

King Louis XIII was born in 1601 in the Louis XIII Salon. It was there that I realized that I had begun to think in terms of Eloi's time or Guillaume's time. I was no longer in the time of kings and queens. This was my culture; I reminded myself to check on which Pelletier had been born close to 1601. I wandered through alone but I also wandered through with my ancestors who would have never been allowed entry.

*Château d'Ecouen* is now the *Musée National le Renaissance* and it may be found in the small town of Ecouen, just north of Paris. The dedication and exaltation to the French monarchy, which was the focus in the building of this castle, was the same devotion as that given in building the church of 1792 when Jean-Baptiste Pelletier was building *Saint-Louis*.

Initially I had walked up to the chateau through the woods that surround it, using the two-kilometre winding path built many years prior. It was early morning, just before the museum's opening, and no one else was to be seen; I imagined myself on this same path during the time of the Renaissance period. It was a beautiful spring day, and as I came through the trees, I was truly awestruck at the site. I had come up a narrow pathway to the top of the hill and in the clearing was the chateau.

To add to this ambiance was the fact that I needed to cross two moats. The first, a newer addition, was at the outer walls of the forest. It had been built by Napoleon. The second was a dry moat in style, with medieval corner guard posts overlooking it. I was not disappointed when I later checked their authenticity. But at that moment, rather than present myself with architectural detail, I enjoyed the feeling of this magnificent view of another time in history. The ornate dormer windows and arches of the chateau presented a picture to me that seemed historically perfect, even more so than the Châteauof Fontainebleau.

Château d'Ecouen was built by Anne de Montmorency, whose family belonged to sixteenth-century nobility, and whose loyalty to both François I and Henry II was continuous and often rewarded with titles and power. Her family had owned the property from 1183 (along with a smaller building) until the period of building this second chateau in 1538. Originally the décor was austere, but with accumulated wealth a warmer atmosphere evolved. Local artists were commissioned for engravings, paintings, tiling, stained glass, huge tapestries, embroidery and objects d'art.

The chateau sits upon a 150-metre-high hill that dominates the small town of Ecouen, and its vast plain below. This expanse, broken by only a few scattered structures, has not changed in overall appearance in over four hundred years. Complete with the moat, watch towers, masonry escarpment and counterscarp walls, the chateau is faithful to all the design principles of the early Renaissance period. Throughout the chateau, the unschooled visitor can be certain that the character of that which is being observed, looks and feels like – *back then*.

Inside, twelve chimney pieces display elaborately painted decoration in the style of the School of Fontainebleau. Three others are of sculpted marble. The library was the last room to be decorated in 1551. With walnut wainscoting, painted panels of gold arabesques, it is incredibly rich and vibrant.

It was Cardinal Richelieu who changed the ownership. The Montmorency family line was made extinct by the execution of Henri II by Richelieu in 1631. Louis XIII, who confiscated the chateau, then gave it to the sister of Henri II. The ensuing years produced many uses under many different owners until as late as 1962, when it was returned to the state for its present purpose.

The history of the chateau made obvious the fact that the entourage of royalty in Europe could be very fickle. Courting favour with kings or queens was a never-ending process, one highly dependent upon their minds and whims. Many families were in similar circumstances as the Montmorency family. It allowed me an understanding of how the Perche forests given to the Pelletier family in the thirteenth century had slipped away without any documentation– the kind of paper-trail we would expect in the twentieth or twenty-first centuries. On the other hand, I felt happy that my ancestors had at least survived as individuals.

I was pleased to find the Musée National le Renaissance displayed art works from the first half of the sixteenth century as well as from the Middle Ages – it connected me with Elio and his father. Yet there was only a faint echo of the transformation in painting that was wrought by the Renaissance throughout Europe. The museum does not attempt to compete with the many collections of others, which was much to my liking– I could focus on my reason for being there in the first place.

I also reminded myself that Jean Pelletier was known for his goblets. He would have had knowledge of much of what I was observing.

The exhibits at this museum proved that the art of stained-glass painting did not decline in the sixteenth century. Medieval forms and the use of colour and technical perfection are found there, with what is considered to be the best-preserved non-ecclesiastical collections of stained glass in France. There is a showing of newly introduced secular subjects, and perfect technique. Much of this kind of window setting had disappeared when the windows either were replaced by wood, or were destroyed in the Revolution- I wished that I knew what Eloi and Guillaume were able to observe. In contemplating furniture, woodcarvings, glazed pottery, ceramics, enamels, glass, and ironworks of the time, I paused reflecting on the possibilities. I still felt that my lack of historical knowledge was causing me to make incorrect assumptions. I needed to know what Jean's goblets were made of in order to reflect properly.

The sixteenth century was a period when all people of all social strata were fascinated with technique. This was evident from their books, instruments, cabinets, furniture and general collections. Originally nearly three thousand types of tools were listed from this period. I was certain, however, that Jean did not use silver or gold. I made a note to myself: "find out what material was used in 1650 for goblets in Quebec." I was later successful.

In being one of the oldest sites coupled with constant upgrades, The Castle of Vincennes illustrated the history of Royal Palaces. It is being reconstructed in a lavish manner. However, my visit to the Chateau d' Ēcouenand its Musée National le Renaissance was perhaps the most rewarding of all the historical sites I have seen in France. It was the only one of the grand palaces that had been accessible to the middle class.

\* \* \*

The exhibits at the *Musée d'Art et traditions populaires*, told the history of rural life in France. I made note that in 1623, in a painting called Colporteur de Livrets, paperback books were being sold to the people of small towns. Peddler of Booklets was the literal translation. From this, I hazarded a guess that in 1641, Guilaume could likely read and write. If that were the case, he had undoubtedly read and understood his contractual obligations when signing on to move to the New World.

French-Canadian immigrant farmers were enjoying a much higher standard of living than their French counterparts – in every century since. In France, as was well presented in this museum, the extreme poverty and crudeness of rural life continued until the twentieth century. A consistent flow of new immigrants to Canada would have given the habitants a communication of the difference in standards of living. The fact of dire poverty continuing in France would have kept my ancestors and their friends quite content. This museum showed the poverty of France and that my quest of observing my ancestor's way of life was more to the point than presented in the museums of Eastern Canada. Now I was now ready to visit the real thing.

# Chapter 16 - Tourouvre

Guillaume Pelletier's home in Bresolettes and his wife Michèle Mabille's hometown of Tourouvre were to be my next stop. The two towns now had a combined population of fewer than 1,655 people.

Finally arriving seemed anticlimactic - I had planned the details of this trip more than any in my life. In Tourouvre my week was to begin at the Hôtel de France, across the street from the St. Aubin Church, an important family location for me. In my planning, however, I had neglected one detail: the hotel was closed on Mondays. On all of its advertising the statement was dominant: "Located on 13 August 1944 Street, the main-street of the town, named in remembrance of the many civilians who had died during the German occupation. On that fateful day, fifty-four homes had been burned in retaliation for the death of a German sentry by Royal Air Force strafing. The flames of Tourouvre had lasted ten days." No mention of Monday closings was made.

I got organized for a Plan B and checked for other possible hotels. With the plan of returning early Tuesday I set out for the larger village of Mortagne du Perche, only a few minutes away. My first stop there was a quaint, antiquated hotel, that had so much ambiance, I decided cost would not be a consideration. To my relief, it was not expensive, especially compared with Paris hotels.

As I later strolled down the narrow streets, I repeatedly had to remind myself that I was not in Quebec. I had read about the likeness in architecture, and that no other two such unique regions could have such a similar appearance. The reality was that at the same time in history many of the buildings had been designed by the same architects and builders. The arched gate of Saint Denis was built in the late twelfth century with rooms added above it in the sixteenth century. There were sixteenth century and seventeenth century townhouses and cloisters identical to those I had seen in Quebec City. I really found it an enjoyable couple of hours of exploring for that reason.

My first stop on Tuesday was the St. Aubin Church in Tourouvre, where Michelle Mabille was baptized on May 20, 1592, and where she wed Guillaume in 1619. The St. Aubin Church, named in honour of the seventh century bishop of Angers, was built in 1481, using as its foundation, the remains of an earlier church built in 1034. The original church had been almost entirely destroyed during the Hundred Year's War of the previous fourteenth century. In addition to its historic value as a church, St. Aubin is also an important monument for the French-Canadian families whose ancestors lived in the area. There are stained-glass windows and plaques in the church honouring the many ancestors of Canadians who had been baptized here. They also honour by name the individual families from Tourouvre who were part of the emigration to Canada. The Belfry doorway dates from 1616.

Two of the church's stained glass windows commemorate the departure of the eighty families that left for New France in the seventeenth century, by way of each window's composition and subject matter. A favourite window shows Julien Mercier, a leader from Tourouvre, pointing into the horizon; nearby, Percherons gaze out upon the bay toward their ship in contemplation of their voyage. It is no coincidence that the window was erected in 1891 by the premier of Quebec, Honoré Mercier, who was a direct descendant of Julien Mercier. Such is often the wonderful evolution of the mixture of history, myth and fact.

Michelle Mabille and Jean Pelletier are listed on a carved stone board, under the heading "*Canadiens Baptises à Tourouvre*", along with their dates of baptism. Like many such plaques, it is also inscribed with the sentiment: "*Je Me Souviens*". Design and construction of the plaque was personally initiated by His Excellency Gérard Pelletier; a descendant of Jean Pelletier; when he was the *Ambassadeur du Canada en France*, in 1977. A fifteenth century painting titled *Adoration des Mages*, has recently been added above the alter. A tapestry is called the *Charité de Tourouvre*; it had been made in 1554.

On my first visit, I spent three hours in the church. I just sat there in silence. Perhaps I was listening to the centuries of history. It tied together my every visit to every ancient church that I had visited in Europe. I had now, in my own way, at last worshipped with my ancestors. I concluded that this is likely the motivation for many people who make similar treks to the churches of Europe. Perhaps I was just one of the few who could experience the journey with such conclusiveness.

My second stop was at the town hall, such that I could ask permission to visit the museum. Across the square from the church is the small museum that houses information and exhibits related to the Percheron emigration to New France between 1634 and 1651. The key to the museum is kept at the town hall, and because of recent changes in security, the police chief was delegated to accompany me. I knew by communicating with other Canadian and American Pelletiers that records of Michelle Mabille's baptism in 1592 and her marriage to Guillaume Pelletier were easily found within the archives.

Inside the museum a large board lists the names of Tourouvians who left from 1634 to 1651. It shows their dates of birth, names of spouses, the area in New France where they ultimately settled, along with the number of children and their date of death. The reason for their departure is also given – for example, being signed on by *La Compagnie des Cent-Associés*, (The Company of 100 Associates of New France).

A small area had re-created the signing room, where contracts between the Percherons and the company were made a formality. The contracts were originally signed in a building called the *Cheval Blanc*, but the building didn't survive the Second World War battles and the occupation.

As if to highlight my journey, the museum displayed two cabinets. The owner of *La Cristerie*, Guillaume Pelletier's home in Bresolettes, had donated them. The signage on the first indicated its contents that were tools found around the former home of the Pelletier family– and that they were the very same tools used by the family in the sixteenth century.

They included hammers, axes, augers and other building equipment. The second glass-covered case held spoons, forks and other kitchen items. I had visited many such displays of kings and queens, with tools and utensils adorned with gold; but this humble display held far more meaning for me.

Tourouvre in 2005 was a town of 1,643 people. It had been described to me by someone who had visited there ten years earlier; as being impossible to reach without renting a car. Simply put, a train to L'Aigle and a #60 bus to Tourouvre will complete the journey. Many things in rural life such as travel became easier. Still only 140 kilometres from Paris, Tourouvre has retained much of its rural charm.

The previous afternoon I had driven into the Perche Forest to Bresolettes, a town that was now a total population of twelve. Like other small communities in France, here, it is now a *Commune du Parc du Perche*, meaning that it is within the park area and its administration. The mayor of the town is a representative of the official park. I had erroneous information that I needed an appointment through the mayor to visit the two sites important to me, but it was much easier than that.

St. Pierre Church dates back to the sixteenth century. To enter its front door, one has to cross the church's cemetery. That next afternoon I had simply climbed over a small fence and read the directions for viewing as the door remained locked. I was to go two houses down and ask for the key from Madame Lambert. Her home was called *Val Marion* after its builder, a tradition I was beginning to realize was common.

On April 7, 1977, His Excellency Gérard Pelletier, then Canadian ambassador to France and a descendant of Guillaume, unveiled a plaque honouring Guillaume and his brother Antoine on the wall of this church. "*Je Me Souviens*" is again inscribed. Throughout the church, the simplicity of its architecture closely emulates the people and their thoughts of its time so well. Also to view and experience were the ancient church pews, weathered and crumbling from age. These evoked an emotion as I sat and waited, almost naively waiting for an ancestor's voice to be heard. The pews were that old and both the location and the ambiance were that clear. The church had been well used until the nineteenth century; however, the pews had been kept in storage for their antique value and now were added back into the sanctuary.

The Bresolletes area had survived with mining supplementing farming until the last part of the nineteenth century. Wars then systematically took away the young men of the town. From the distant time of Guillaume, coal being produced in the area had been a mainstay. Industry in northern France relied on the local production up until 1880.

My second stop was La Cristerie, Guillaume Pelletier's home. La Cristerie is a corruption of the original name of La Grisetterie, which itself came from the builder, a man by the name of Griset. A welcoming sign on the gate read in French, "This house has a story." It then goes on to describe the odyssey of the Pelletier family.

The current resident is Jacqueline Pelletier-Gaudet. She rents the property from the owner, who had made renovations in 1999. Jacqueline was born in Quebec and educated as a nurse. In1986, she met and had married André Gaudet. Upon my having knocked on the door, she opened the top portion only- older homes in France use this type of door/window combination. It looks very practical. When I announced I was a Pelletier, she invited me in without hesitation.

Immediately upon entering, I could view the original frame work and the incredible flint-stone walls, called silex by the French. From the appearance of the framework, it was evident that the original house was half-timbered, as were a great many houses in Normandy and Quebec. The original portion of the house, the central part between two chimneys dates back to the sixteenth century. The main beams in the bedroom and living room are from the original post-and-beam structure. The original hearth is now part of the bedroom. I could see why the fireplace wall had been retained: on each side of the hearth there was a large rectangular pillar of granite - solid and not moveable without a major undertaking. This massive wall is also viewed from the exterior and it dates back to the sixteenth century– a time when Guillaume and his younger brother Antoine would have spent their early childhood playing in this bright sunlit yard.

After my visit of almost an hour, Jacqueline brought out a Pelletier guest book, which I very happily signed. She had lost her husband André Gaudet, only one year earlier. Funeral services were held in the same village church that I had just visited. In leaving, I offered a payment, which she strongly declined. She was living there as a *caretaker of tradition*, and I am very thankful. She understood my journey and I think I understand her dedication.

I had booked into the Hôtel de France in Tourouvre in the morning and now had some leisure time to explore the region. It was a short drive to see La Grande Trappe, the original Trappist monastery dating from 1140 in the neighbouring village of Soligny. This was another dimension of thought for me, deeply rooted as I was in the probabilities of life in the 1550s. I couldn't conceive of the Trappist monks being of any significance to the Pelletier family, although they lived so close in the same forested area. I drove slowly and focused on the forest. Winding paved roads welcomed tourists, with many being on bicycles, as they enjoyed the casually rolling hills. Coming from a land of tall cedars, I found the trees of the forest to be bushes, however they were consistently laced with Renaissance architecture. Near the buildings I could view a few small groves of balsam fir and stately oak trees. It was a casual drive through time.

I spent most of one day in the Bresolettes forest, and of that I am very glad. I had paused, as it was necessary to do in order to contemplate my ancestors. This could not be a quick drive-through. I knew later in the whirlwind of Paris, I would not regret this time of reflection in my family's footsteps.

That evening I savoured a meal of local dishes at my hotel. I sampled a small crock of rillettes, a hard cider with red currant cassis. A Perche specialty is *boudin noir*, which is a blood sausage or black pudding, pan-fried with apples. It was delicious. My meal, however, wasn't completely authentic to being local – it was lacking a bottle of local French wine. Unfortunately the acidic soil of this area of the former Perche province doesn't allow grapes for wine to be grown here. The hotel owners were a very friendly couple and thoroughly engaging. They appeared equally at ease behind the administration desk, in the dining room and in the kitchen preparing meals.

As my exquisite meal was drawing to a close, I asked the proverbial question of, "What time is the restaurant open for breakfast?"

"What time will you be up for breakfast?" the owner responded.

"About 8:30."

"Perfect," he said. "We open at 8:30". As I was the only guest in this hotel for dinner, I was also the only guest for breakfast. Some things work out fine.

At the hotel we talked about a lot of things and the history of Tourouve was the hotel owner's favourite topic. He left me talking with his wife for a few moments and returned with a stack of brochures, the contents of which he knew by heart. In 920 Rollon the first Duke of Normandy, ruled as one of the first seigneurs of Tourouvre, along with his wife Gisèle. The crest and shield of Tourouvre show this local history. They also show three leaves of the Canadian maple tree in recalling the eighty families that left Tourouvre in the 1640s for a better life.

By now, I had discovered that the father of Elio was René Pelletier, who had married Marie Cupit in Bresolettes. There was a distinct possibility that he was from Chartres, the next and last stop on my journey of family history in France. Chartres had been a major centre when Réne left there. First, I would come to know well the small town of Bresolettes, located idyllically in these quiet hills and not of great significance to France's national history, but of profound importance to me.

It was now clear as to why Percherons had been chosen to settle in Canada. They were all attached to the land, as farmers, fishermen, artisans and labourers and they were well experienced with generations having worked in hard labour. By

2004, six families of New France – 250 people – had grown to one and a half million descendants.

A part of me will always remain in Bresolletes. The view from that ancient family home as it sits serenely overlooking a verdant Perche valley is not merely a tourist's photograph, but a memory that will never lose its vividness. The walk up to my ancestral home, by way of a path unchanged through the centuries, is indelibly etched in my mind's eye. To stand before the hearth of the great stone fireplace that they had so painstakingly built was a once-in-a-lifetime experience. Its hardy survival of the elements, decade upon decade, mirrored the tenacity of the surviving generations.

To have followed the 500-year-old path of the family has been one of the greatest treasures life has given me. It is my hope that everyone – of every generation– may find the daring to examine their own history and discover its meaning as I did – for pride in one's heritage is a wonderful thing.

# PELLETIER FAMILY CHRONOLOGY
# - 500 YEARS

## 1 - IN CHARTRES

Rene Pelletier Married Marie Cupit. He was a descendant of Barthelemy Le Pelletier of Brittany (had lived in the 1300's).
Visited Site:

> Chartres, Eure-et-Loire, France.

## 2 - THE MAN OF FRENCH ANTIQUITY

Eloi Pelletier (d. 1640) Married Françoise Matte.
Visited Site:

> La Christerie, in Bresolettes, Orne, France.

## 3 - THE PIONEER

Guillaume Pelletier (1598-1657) from Bresolettes, Married Michelle Mabille (1592-1665).
Only surviving Child: Jean.
Visited Sites:

> (a) St. Aubin church, Tourouvre, Orne, France.
> (b) Montmorency Falls Park, Beauport, Quebec, adjacent to the first Pelletier farm of 1644 to 1676.

## 4 - THE ARTIST

Jean Pelletier (1627-1698) Married Anne Langlois (1637-1704) in 1649 in Beauport, Quebec.
Children: Noel, Anne, Rene, Antoine, Jean, Marie- Delphine, Marie, Charles, Charlotte.
Visited Sites:

> (a) St. Aubin church, Tourouvre, Orne, France.
> (b) Jean's farm of 1663 to 1667 at
> 693-697 chemin Royal, Ile D'Orleans, Quebec, Canada.
> (c) The tombstone of Jean and Anne Pelletier, at
> Riviere Quelle, Quebec, Canada, just off Hwy 132.

## 5 - THE PATERNAL PARENT

Charles Pelletier (1671-1748) Married (1) Terese Quel (2) Marie-Barbe St. Pierre at Riviere-Quelle, Quebec. Children from 2nd marriage: Jean-Bernard, François, Marie-Barbe, Gabriel, Jacques, Marie-Rosalie, Marie-Reine, Marie-Francoise, Marie-Anne, Pierre.
Visited Sites :

>The Pelletier farm of 1679 to 1757, at
>Pelletier Street, St. Roch des Aulnaies, Quebec.

## 6 - THE FARMER

Pierre Pelletier (1731-1801) Married Marie-Madeleine Lebel (1734-1773).
Children Catherine, Genevieve, Jean-François, Marthe, Madeleine, Rosalie, Marie-des-Anges, Angélique, Jean-Pierre, Pierre-Basile, Jean-Baptiste, Germain.
Visited Sites:

>The monument to the Jean Pelletier families at
>La Seigneurie des Aulnaies, Quebec.

## 7 - THE MEDIEVAL TRADITIONALIST

Jean-Baptiste Pelletier (1768-1825) Married (1) Madeleine Pellerin (2) Judith St. Pierre-dit-Desein.
Children from (1) Rose, Marie-Louise, Angelique, Constance, Jean-Baptiste, Celestin, Francois, Zephirin.
Visited Sites:

>*St. Louis Church* built by Jean- Baptiste Pelletier in
>1792, with his marriage in 1793 there, at
>St. Roch-des- Aulnaies, Québec.

## 8 - THE REBEL PHILOSOPHER

Célestin Pelletier (1801-1865) Married Justine Aubut. Moved to New Brunswick as a Blacksmith.
Children: Rémi, Joseph, Alphonse, Thomas.
Visited Sites:

    (a) The Kamouraska museum, farm and blacksmith shop from 1757 to 1827.
    (b) Pelletier Street (former farm), St. Basile, New Brunswick.

## 9 - THE RENAISSANCE MAN

Rémi Pelletier (1840-1900) Married Philomene Martin.
Children: Henry, Stanislaus, Ernestine, Alfred, George, Joseph.
Visited Sites:

    The Pelletier Mill from 1880 to 1919, on Pelletier Road, Pelletier Mill district, New Brunswick.

## 10 - THE ROOTS SEEKER

Stanislaus (Stanley) Claude Pelletier (1866-1939).
Married Edith Flavie Daigle (1875-1909.
Children: Arthur (Art), Paul-Emile, Edith, Yvonne, Denis (Jeff) Albertine, Eva (m. Roberts).
Visited Sites:

    (a) Edith Daigle 1948 home, museum, New Brunswick.
    (b) Grand'Pre museum, Nova Scotia.
    (c) Carequet, New Brunswick, an *Acadian* town.
    (d) Hotel Dieu de Saint Joseph (school), St. Basil, NB.
    (e) Pelletier Lumber Mill, Coleman, Alberta, Hwy #3.

## 11 - THE SUBTLE COMIC

Paul-Emile Pelletier (1899-1955) Married Yvonne Roberts in Dawson Creek, BC. Son: Lonnie.
Visited Sites:

    South Dawson, BC - the two valley farms.

## 12 - THE AUTHOR

Lonnie Paul Pelletier, born in 1943 in Dawson Creek, BC. I have lived most of my life in Vancouver, BC. I am an author and a painter. I had spent three decades in Real Estate Management.

## 13 - FUTURE GENERATIONS

Christie Anne Pelletier, born in 1979 in Vancouver and Jeffrey Paul Pelletier, in 1981, in Vancouver.

Christie is in Real Estate Management.

The world of Jeff Pelletier is that of twenty-second century technology as he pursues his occupation of video producer and CEO in Vancouver, BC, Canada.

## 14 - FUTURE GENERATIONS

Salvador and Christie's son Leonardo Ascencio Pelletier was born August 17, 2009 in Vancouver, BC - residing in Mexico where traditionally the son takes the name of the mother.

No bibliography is appended. I soon found, when the time came to prepare one, that the point of no return had been reached. My list of over one thousand items, including history books, papers, extracts, manuscripts, and display and archived museum items would be so daunting that its value would be negligible. The historical information used has become a matter of clichés, with no possible credit being available for the first analyzed facts, all of which may be found in any library or on the world-wide web.

Thank you for reading my book.
A link to my web pages presenting my
other books and eBooks is

# http://LonPelletier.com

**LONNIE PELLETIER ART & WRITING**

125 of my paintings (as the *art of outer space*) are also shown as slide shows at my web site.

www.ingramcontent.com/pod-product-compliance
Lightning Source LLC
Chambersburg PA
CBHW072126270326
41931CB00010B/1688